THROUGH
IMMORTAL SHADOWS
SINGING

THROUGH IMMORTAL SHADOWS SINGING
Copyright © Mari Ness 2017
All Rights Reserved.

ISBN 978 1 907881 55 8

Papaveria Press.
West Yorkshire, UK.
Printed in England.
www.papaveria.com

Except in the case of quotations embedded in critical articles or reviews, no part of this book may be reproduced or transmitted in any form or by any means, electronic or mechanical, including photocopying, recording, or by any information storage and retrieval system, without permission in writing from the publisher.

Mari Ness has asserted her moral right to be identified as the author of this work.

Through Immortal Shadows Singing

Mari Ness

Papaveria Press

THROUGH IMMORTAL SHADOWS SINGING

MARI NESS

PAPAVERIA PRESS

CONTENTS

7 | EOS
10 | THAUMA
20 | THESEUS
23 | FATA
24 | HIMEROS
28 | GAMOS
31 | PEITHO
37 | DIOSCURI
40 | PAREGORON
42 | BRIBES
45 | TROY
52 | WAR
55 | PROTOS
62 | DEUTEROS
69 | TRITOS
75 | TETARTOS
85 | PEMPTOS
86 | ECTOS
93 | EBDOMOS
98 | OGDOOS
105 | EVATOS
126 | DEKATOS
127 | THANATOS
134 | DITHYRAMB
138 | O IPPOS
142 | EGYPT
148 | RETURN
161 | DAEMON

EOS

My mother taught me of the use of drugs
the smoke that could entrap the wise
in dreams of their own making, the herbs
that could bring sweet peaceful rest
or stop the heart, the leaves
that could bring joyfulness or calm
or death. I mixed the powders beneath her eye,
and tried them on my tongue, and watched
her feathered hands drop sweet comfort
into her husband's wine.
This, my sweets, is power, she said
as she slowly mixed the wine
with a rich green powder, deftly
keeping my sister's fingers
out of sweet mischief. *Power
to transform a man. Or woman. If you
wish.* I watched the wine bubble and hiss. *Truly?*
I said, knowing all too well
that sometimes adults lie. *Truly,* she said,
and smiled. *How else do you think
I could have captured
that white swan?*

These days, people wander by
demanding to see the fragments of the eggs:
the egg of stone and the egg of gold
where, they say,
we nestled in safety before our births,
the four of us, of no woman born,
before we crept away from our shells.
I have even heard a few clever souls
showing credulous folk small

fragments of a brittle stone
they claim caressed my sister's skin.
I, of course, they claim and tell,
was wrapped within the shell of gold.

No one remembers birth, of course:
even I, god-kissed, as they name me, and cursed
with undying memory, I
cannot tell if I crawled into the sun
from a mother's womb, or from an egg –
but I think it was the first. I remember
my mother's feathered hands
caressing my softened cheeks, and
remember the way my mother's body
would swell and shrink, just as a woman's would
and the way her eyes would follow us –
not the eyes of a woman who would have left
children bound in eggs of stone and gold.

And whatever the songs may sing,
naming me daughter of gods, of Zeus,
I tell you I am all too mortal in my pain,
all too laced with agony. They claim
the gods can suffer as mortals do, but I –
I have seen them, and I know that is
but a tale believed by mortal men. The gods can suffer,
yes, and weep, but more –
that pain they leave to humans to bear,
while they watch smiling.

Always this is said of me: men fought for me,
men died for me. More is told of this than of
the golden home I formed in Sparta,
the home I built with my hands and voice,
that many said could house the very gods.
The one thing of my work, my own. But none
speak of this first. Always I am

what I am to men, the woman standing
on the burning walls, the woman watching
men wrestle in the mud, the woman hiding
as men clashed their swords. Men fought for me,
men died for me. My name made heroes
of mortal men, my eyes chased their very destinies.
And yet, when caught in battle rage
they never saw, nor spoke, of me at all.

I see swans, I see swans
I hunger for the weight of wings,
for feathers to steal me into song.

Ask not for consistency in my tale.
Memory is more fleeting than a swift rabbit
darting from the jaws of a fox, or a morning rain
sucked up by the summer sun.
And my tale of grief and madness,
has so much to remember.
And forget.

I am abducted, abductor,
lover and wife, chaste
and whore. About me coil
a thousand songs, a thousand lies,
and even this song may be a lie,
a song I whisper
to take command of my own tale.

THAUMA

In later days, so I have heard
immortals could only be glimpsed
in the edges of twilight and shadow,
or in the cold light cast
by the immortal shifting moon,
shimmering through the trees
to trick the eyes to *other*, or sometimes
deep within a wood lost
to all mortal human sound.
Not so with us. We glimpsed the gods
feasting in the skies; saw them laughing
in our halls; heard them whisper in our ears;
and witnessed a shifting of their eyes,
the slightest movement of their hands,
the sudden shifting of merciless fate,
bent to the whims of immortal boredom,
caught in their endless whirlwinds
of quarreling and dance.

We tried to coax them from the woods,
the dancing shadows and singing trees,
the springs that leapt at mortal song,
entrancing mortals into their golden realms.
But they would only be summoned with a song,
and I, I could not sing,
and my mortal sister, my beloved twin, would not.

I want a god, declared my sister,
biting proudly into an apple red
with heat. *A god to suckle on my breasts.*

She laughed. *They say it is nothing
like a man. They say with the gods
the night truly lives, that the twilight
comes alive.*

My mother wrapped a golden veil
about her face. *They say the truth.
They twist into trees, the lovers of gods,*
my mother said, weaving rich red robes,
*or die beneath their flames, weeping as
new gods are ripped from their thighs.*
I have learnt to cherish well
the unsteady sounds of mortal breaths
in the flickering twilight shadows.

> Oh, hold your love for mortal men,
> hold your love, my daughters,
> hold your love for mortal men,
> and waste it not upon the
> fickleness of gods.

Her eyes lingered on my mortal father's form,
as he worked upon his swords. Thunder pounded,
and bowing, we said nothing
of the equal fickleness of men.

Two bronze mirrors were our brother twins,
fooling eye and ear. But not us, though we too
bore the name of twin: My sister
slimmer than I, dark of eye and hair, yet white –
a skin so pale it seemed her skin
had stolen the light of the moon.
Like her mother, the whispers said, and indeed
my mortal father's reddened eyes
lingered long upon my sister's form,
and watched her enter the sea,
eyes devouring the linen clinging to her skin.

And I, gold, golden, made of gold,
my skin shimmering in the light of the sun,
dimming at the mere approach
of thunder in the hills.

We walked along the stony hills and
through the olive groves, she the swift leader,
I her golden shadow. Sometimes we saw *them*,
my other sisters, other cousins
dancing between the trees and air,
twisting themselves new forms from water. That is –
I saw them, and whispered greetings. Her
pale face admitted nothing, admitted
no other sisters of my blood,
save the other mortal ones we shared, though to us
those three sisters were never more
than noisy shadows, voices to be fled,
burdens to be cared for, toys to be dropped
when the songs of forests and seas
called to us, or when our brothers, yelling
pulled us to practice arts of war.

———

My brothers, my brothers:
so far off these memories that I know not
if now I sing as I remember,
or as I remember the songs.

Even in Troy they sang of them both,
and in Sparta – oh Sparta – a day
was never without their songs.

———

We followed them, as sisters would,
to join their games of war and rage,
fighting with shouts and sticks.
They abandoned us, as brothers would

to their own games and plays,
until the hands of girls were needed,
or until one of us raised their thunder.
A thunder united. For no one watching, would know
that one was born to death, and one
to dance among the stars, or in
the great immortal halls
clustered atop the highest mountains.
That one held thunder in his veins,
and the other mere mortal blood,
for their fury rang as one,
a single clash of lightning.
Far otherwise with my sister, my twin, and me.

———

So slow, so slow, that loss,
I cannot tell you where it began
or where it ended. So dark, so dark,
that loss, that even now,
in the dry lands, I find it
robbing me of sight.

———

Two small girls upon a silken bed,
hand in hand, dream in dream:

Two sisters watching the Spartan men,
and listening to whispers.

Helen, Helen, whisper the men.
Clytemnestra, Clytemnestra, whispers the king.

The secret dances. The touch of hands.
The growing anger in my sister's eyes.

She stands in the shadows of the king.
So strong, so strong, the king's hard hands.

So hard upon her slim shoulders.

He does not touch me, the king.

Who sees the bruises in the dark?
Or beneath the fine linens of a princess,
my sister, my twin?

The men of the court watch me in hunger, hunger.

Anger fills my sister's eyes.
I would that I were you.
I might have answered her this truth:
I would that I were her.

Instead I retreated into the corners,
where the shadows might hide my golden skin,
knowing no answer I might make
could be heard above that rising rage.

———

They watched me as I paced down their streets,
golden, princess, future queen,
my hand clasped tightly upon an olive branch,
or holding a wreath of flowers and leaves.
Gold trailed behind me, marking my steps,
and they watched, the Spartans, watched
in uncheering silence until my sister, my twin,
pulled at my hand, and dragged me to the hills,
where laughing we chased each other over stones
and merrily begged for songs from shadows.

———

Child of thunder, child of swans, they said,
though my feet were rooted deep within the earth,
and I could no more fly than could a mouse
fleeing the fierce claws of a swooping hawk.

She walks in lightning, or so they said,
even as I sat forlorn and wished
for but a taste of lightning's power.

Cold, cold, this land.
Dry, dry, my lips.
My teeth chatter
as old bones in a pot,
robbed of all marrow.

The webs of women, my mother said, and so she taught
the arts of loom and thread, of spindle and warp,
that as queens our walls might gleam
with woven webs, that as princesses our gowns might shine
as those of the very gods. *The needs of women*, our brothers said,
and so they taught us of knives and fists.
Our needs as women, my sister said, gazing into my golden face,
watching others watch me with hungry eyes.
Stealing me to twilight shadows,
she tried to learn what made me *different*,
and I tried to learn what would make me *same*.

Golden, they named my voice, golden as
my skin and hair, golden as the sandals
that bedecked my feet. A lie. A lie.
But no more than the other lies
that danced about my ears.

But still a lie. Alone of all my mother's children
I could not sing. My fingers could
dance upon the harp and lyre;
my golden feet could drum in any dance,
and all singers called to my pounding blood.

But from my throat no tune emerged,
only the sound of roughened stone, or
the throbbing of a flying swan.
Teach me to sing, I begged, I begged,
opening my throat to honeyed drinks,
and governing my every breath. *Teach me.*
My mother's hands rested in
my golden hair. *It is not a gift
for all.* In a corner, shadows laughed,
and behind me, the voice of my sister, my twin
raised in glorious and perfect song.

And so I turned to shadows for song.
Could I catch one, and place it in my throat –
the singing shadows of the woods, whose songs
darted upon the wind from leaf to leaf,
mingled with the calls of birds so that
uncertain hearers might not know
who had called: immortal, ghost or bird –
could I catch one, and place in it my throat,
then, then I might sing. Or if not –
I might, I might learn their shadowsong.

And as I waited for a song of shadow,
I strummed my harp as others sang,
and immortals crept close to hear
their divinely mortal voices.

So clearly they dance now in my mind:
the roughened faces of the spirits of trees,
the merry faces of trickster fauns,
the ever changing beauty of
the naiads of water, rising up
from stream and spring, to laugh as we leapt
from hill to hill and tree to tree.
So clearly now. My mind twists, changes,
building ghosts from shadows.

Two gates before me, of ivory and horn.
I pause, extend a trembling hand
to caress the horn, to hear its silent song.

Always they watched: the golden light
pouring from my skin and hair,
my very steps, my every move. Always they watched.
They brought children to stare at me,
so that they might tell of golden Helen
playing with her toys. Always they whispered,
and muttered prayers and spells,
and clutched rough scrolls from distant Egypt,
and luck stones from more nearby lands.
Thunder. Thunder. *The lightning
rests in her skin.*

Always, always, the sound of songs.
They dance with thunder, some sang in joy.
As others answered: *Too close. Too close.
To thunder. And to rage.*

They sang, they said, of my fierce brothers.
But their eyes watched me as they sang.

Never have I known what it is
not to be watched. Not to walk in beauty,
draped so deeply in its folds
that few could see beyond its light. Not to hold
golden light within my hands, spilling it
as other women might spill water. Not to feel myself

apart, alone, even as I felt
all too mortal hungers, all too mortal pains,
all too mortal need of sleep, and cried
all too mortal tears, which drained
the golden light from my face.

No mortal stands easy near a child of thunder, they said,
and in turn I say this: no child of thunder stands easy
beneath ever watching mortal eyes.

When thunder rumbled in the hills, my mother smiled
and drew me close. *Your father's rage. They say
he has a most uneasy temper, hottest
of all immortals, even those
who play and dance with fire,
or know the anger of the sea.
They say it is his endless sight
that drives his fury, that sends his lightning
tumbling into mortal trees.*

                               Does he see me?

Silence. The crackling of thunder.
The gathering of shadows. Her hands
tight upon my arms, the feathers
digging into my skin. *Oh, my daughter,
that he does, he does.*

I do not recall
my mother's death –
the rush of wings, the call of thunder
the sudden silence
and the falling of rain.

But that she died, I know all too well.

I knew it in the absence of her voice.
I knew it in the silence of the swans.

Swift, so swift, the change of years:
Herons raising wings into the wind –
one moment fishing, and the next –
no more than ripples in the water
to mark their sudden passage.

Inside my mind, words tumble, tumble –
I reach for a word, pluck it
like a child with a slender harp
uncertain of where the song should go.

I said I knew love, oh love.
My feet shiver on these barren stones.
Sisters, brothers, mother, and thunder –
but this is not the love you meant.
I hunger, I hunger.
Let me tell you of that first love.

THESEUS

Why do you shake? I turned from him
and closed my eyes
to the sight of a bull-masked man.

Whatever they may say, Theseus
was not unkind. He said.
He would be my armor, my shield,
against my own beauty, that danger,
that threat to my slender throat.
I remembered the way
my sister's eyes *burned*, and shivered
against him. He stroked
my throat

                                        and spoke
of the minotaur's hot stinking breath, of
drawing a string against its throat, of feeling
the thread cut into his fingers, of pulling and pulling
against the blood in his hands. Of finding
no monster, nor even a bull:
merely a man choked beneath
a clay fired mask. A man with less
divinity than he. Of lifting the fragile girl
in his arms, of resting his lips
upon her soft neck, of placing her upon
a bed of dark flowers, of leaving her in
the sweet embrace
of a drunken god.

Sometimes he thought she

came to him, shining,
dripping with wine.

Sometimes he dreamed he
sipped honeyed wine
from her nipples,
her lips.

I held him as he cried, and cried.

Only with the touch of gods
did he weep, he said.
Golden power
shimmered through
my hands. I questioned
his tears
with my lips
on his neck.

So young I was.
So young.

I shivered against
his thieving hands.

He would hold me, hold me,
against all gods and men,
he said, for he grasped
my golden skin, my
godlit eyes. He was
a son of the sea,
and he stormed,
he stormed.

I am not he, my lover said,
moving against me. *I am no bull,
no clay masked man, no slayer of monsters.*

*My blood holds no storms, only
the clouds. I cannot hold you
against gods and men.*

My breasts tingled. I watched him
with wary eyes. Eyes hidden, he
bent to my breasts.
*I would drink this instead
of honeyed wine.*

———※———

Dreams crackle into dust,
swirl and settle upon my feet.
I breathe, I breathe, this stuff of dreams,
and feel a dryness in my throat.

———※———

In time, my brothers returned me,
weighted down with silver chains,
to my father's mighty halls, to linger
in my mortal father's halls, and wait.
Wait, as he called for mortal men,
for self-named heroes of mortal blood,
as great as Theseus, he whispered,
or greater. Suitors would come,
they told me. Suitors would come.
And with them feasts of plenty,
and new dresses of linen and silk.
I remembered Theseus' lips
upon my own, and wished
the light upon my skin would dim,
as I shivered in the shadows.

FATA

I walk, knowing that the queen of death
may name me sister, that the
cry of the hunt
shares my blood, that I share a father
with the Fates.

They are pitiless, my sisters, pitiless
in their spinning, and not all my cries
nor claims of blood
can halt their knives in flight.

I leave blood drops on the ivory gates,
a small payment for my passage,
and the songs lost between them.

Always, always, the waiting,
of knowing my fate within the hands of men,
immortal and mortal alike,
to pace in endless wondering
along stone and wooden floors,
to the sound of distant thunder
and a goddess' nearby laughter.

Always, always, the knowing:
that I would take my fate,
and with it, make my song my own.

HIMEROS

Fifty suitors, or a hundred, or ten:
I did not count, though my sister did,
peering between the columns of our hall,
marking white lines on a dark rock,
to piss upon, or toss into the sea.
Fifty suitors. I did not mark their faces,
though my brothers did, fingering
fine bows. A hundred suitors:
the man I called father sighed,
placing a fist between his eyes. And more:
each man of every hill, demanding
his chance at the divine.

Men could, those days, find other loves
enchanted by an immortal's touch:
green girls laughing from their trees,
corn maidens whose swift love,
would last but one golden summer,
water women, with songs so sweet
men could not hear their own swift deaths.
And yet to me these men all came,
standing in our wooden halls,
demanding to see my golden skin,
demanding to watch me dance,
to have one sight, one touch,
to drag the divine from my veins.
Safer than immortal waters, safer than the
laughing gods, who might
seize a life with but a thought,
or drown it beneath a sudden river.
And yet, it was I, mortal and divine,
who brought these men to bloody deaths.

I press gold against my lips,
and sip a drop of silver light.

I knew much of the wrath of Love,
of how she had turned a scornful girl
into the lover of a bear, of how she had turned
another woman into true stone. I knew much
of the wars of Love, of how she had quarreled
with the Queen of Death (another sister, another queen)
for possession of a certain boy.
But of Love, I knew little at all.

Even hidden by columns,
covered in shadows,
never was I free
of the gaze of men,
the tracking eyes
that held my breasts, my feet, my hair,
the quickened breaths that filled my ears.
Such the price of beauty.
Such the price of immortal blood,
running through my mortal veins.

Do not take that one. The voice of my sister,
my twin, harsh in its anger. *Any but him.*
I peered about the columns, searching
the lines of men, to find the one
that had seized her gaze: the grimmest of lions,
the sternest of men. He had not even caught my eye
in truth, but I turned a golden smile upon my twin.

And why should I not?

The softest ringing of metal upon a stone.
The swiftest turning beneath her cloak.
Alone, alone, with nothing but shadows and red columns:

And I looked upon grim Agamemnon.

My sister watched as maids draped me in gold,
watched my feet slide in golden sandals,
so cold upon my feet, watched my hands
fall beneath the weight of coins. The man I called father
shouted his wealth beneath the pelting golden rain.
The suitors watched, eyes hungering.
The ghosts of angry hands
closed about my throat.

Through the dry sands I walk and walk,
searching, searching.
I imagine the shadow of a hawk,
and take comfort in its wings.

He found me in the corners, crouching from my suitors;
he found me hidden behind the red columns
that pushed the roof against the sun,
protecting the gods from that heated wrath.
He found me, and said no word,
and so, wordless, I married him, my lover, my king,
in the quietness of spring,
in the harshness of sea-salt winds,
as seals shrieked in nearby waves,
telling of their unfathomable dives.

The lesser heroes watched me glide on golden floors,
muttering tales of Heracles, and the son of the sea
who had placed his hands about my throat.
They watched my brothers string their bows.
They swore, and swore, and swore again.

In the quietness of spring, she drew me back
to the olive trees and hills, to the shadows
of the mountains. We rested our feet
in a shadowed spring, watching the water
pool beneath our legs, waiting for
a water nymph to rise and sing, or a water god
to cover us in shadows.

*You were not the only one
to feel the touch of a man*, whispered my sister,
my twin, baring her breasts to me. *Not the only
to know desire.* Upon her pale wrists dangled
golden bracelets, heavy with lapis
its dark blue unsoothing to the eye.
They fell together with a dull sound,
clicking as she walked. *But the only one
not to bear a child. The only one
not to see your child die.*

My hand reached out, dripping golden light.
I placed a finger upon her arm.

*The brother of your lover, your king.
He snatched my child from my arms.
I think I am to wed him.*

Still, still, was the water below us.
Quiet, quiet, the birds above.
Hungry, hungry, the earth below.

GAMOS

In the quietness of spring, I heard their song,
ringing blessings upon my marriage, my love:
Timandra, Phoebe and Philonoe singing,
and above them all, the voice of my sister, my twin,
purer than the light of the gods,
more piercing than the fiercest spear
in the hands of an angry god.

I opened my mouth, but sang no word;
reached trembling hands for a harp not there,
and shook in the coldness of their song.

Dry, dry, the dust of dreams.
Cold, cold my feet in these sands.

Some name me daughter of Nemesis,
daughter of Night, though golden light
never left my hands, and never did Night
wrap me in her dark safety –
a protection I found only in light and fire.

But I know nights, I know nights,
where the slender fingers of
tender night brought more than comfort,
more than love.
I know nights, I know nights.
I cling to them in the sounds of thunder.

The speed, the speed, the speed of love!
Swift as lightning crackling upon the churning waves,
or slow as long stored honey poured out upon grain,
drop by careful drop, a hint of sweetness
still to come.

What can I say of my love, my king,
that history and song
has not shaped into a lie? More maligned, indeed,
even than my lover, my prince, and many more
who now wail in the wretched chains
lost beneath the earth, and more praised
than some that might have wrestled
deeper deeds and monsters
from the groaning earth.

Gentle, he was, gentle, and full of laughter,
save when he raised his voice in cries of war,
and shook his spear upon the fields of battle.
Always, always, beneath the shadow,
of that so furied king, his brother,
always, always, attempting to lighten
that fury, that rage, with the softness of laughter.
Gentle, gentle, with the great Achilles,
joking even with that trickster king,
a quiet voice among my suitors,
until I heard his shouts of laughter,
until he had me aching with his jests,
and if I turned from him at first,
it was from no deed of voice or hand
but merely the presence of those shadowy hands
that lingered by my throat.

The touch of his skin calls to me, calls,
and I ache, I ache in the darkness.

He touched me, and I remembered *trust*.
I stepped back, Theseus's ghostly hands
upon my neck. His eyes flickered,
and he bowed. I would not love my king.
Not then.

PEITHO

He came to me at court, my prince,
shining in silver and bronze, he came,
and knelt at the feet of my king,
watching my slender ankles. My king
declined his gifts of gold, and asked
him for a laughing song. My prince bowed,
and sang fair tunes, and I watched
them both, as my skin burned.

When my love, my king, left to walk among the olives,
when my sister, my twin, had left to rest beneath her shadows,
he came to me, my prince, my love,
he came to rest upon my feet, and
sing songs of golden lands and laughing gods.
My fingers stroked his golden harp,
lingering upon its strings.
They trembled in my hands,
yielding their fragile notes
with but a touch of skin. He laughed
at my tentative touch, bid me
stroke the strings more boldly.
My fingers ran across the harp,
and we trembled as it burst into song.

The dark webs of love lace themselves
upon my skin, and tighten, tighten.
I raise my hands to my cheeks,
and try to remember breath.

When did his lips
first touch mine? I cannot tell –
the lightest brush across my cheek –
a salute half imagined, only half felt.
Fingers brushing my lips. His own
grazing my hands as if
a careless spirit had
moved them there,
no more than a touch,
less than a thought.
Until in the shadows
our lips were joined,
pulled there by some unknown god,
caught helpless in that grasp.
That, oh that,
I remember.

In the waters of Acheron, I swim, I swim,
exulting in the cold, diving to the depths,
the waters tight about me, like a newfound lover,
molding the river to my skin.

I spent that night with my lover, the king,
caressing his skin, tasting his tongue,
the warm hands of the goddess
still dancing upon my skin.

The memory of love
leaves me unwarmed.
I shiver, shiver in the sands.

Through the columns, my prince eased towards me,
dragging me to darker corners and softer shadows.
(And already he was my prince; I knew not how,
but mine, mine: those words slipped through, the way sand
slides through open hands.) We sat upon silken cushions,
and spoke of the journeys that distant thread had travelled,
through the very lands of gods and monsters,
to shimmer beneath sun and shadow. We spoke of
cities we had never seen, mountains we had
never climbed, pathways we had not walked.
I would show you Troy, he said. *The topless towers –*
that still grow and grow, though men fear
that already we challenge the bright gods.
They anger swiftly. As you might know.
The swiftest of glances at my hands
still filled with golden light. *I still marvel*
after three filled years of standing on their summits.
I would show you Troy. And its mountains.
And the forests and their springs.

A sudden longing stole over me,
winding its way across throat and heart,
a longing foreign yet familiar. Golden light pulsed
upon my neck. I looked at Sparta, stony Sparta,
firm with mud and slaves, of the cities I
had never seen, trapped behind Sparta's thick walls.

There is another, I said, with nervous breath.
He smiled. *And for me as well.* His hands reached
across the cool green marble. *Can you come*
for but a visit? Our cities might trade. And the seas –
the seas are dark and cool. I would have
you see the dance of the seafoam.
Our tongues met, quite by accident
it seemed. His light touch lingered on my breast.
A visit, I murmured. *A mere visit.* Golden light

pressed on my chest, my head. I withdrew my mouth.
A visit, and wondered why this word
felt so full of truth and lies at once.

Have you ever drunk the dust of dreams,
tasted the horrors of unwaking night,
the wonders of unfettered thought,
where even mortals can do the deeds of gods?

I did not know of that dark vow,
the words woven by that trickster king,
that should I ever leave my king,
should I ever be taken from his halls,
that they would follow, one by one,
that they would challenge the wine-dark seas,
and plunge their swords on foreign sands.

Hated, I am, hated,
they tell me, and I see
the truth in their eyes,
the eyes of every woman,
the eyes of every child.
I did not ask for war,
I whisper, unheard,
knowing it would not matter
if they heard.

In my time women danced
between two loves, or sometimes three,
mortals and sweet gods. They
held the rushing river between their thighs

and filled the mouths of mortal lovers
with the sweetest wines. *Beds are meant
for sharing*, whispered my sister, my twin
as she danced beneath Agamemmon's frown.
Even virgins danced
with gods and fire. I –
I had two loves, two lovers –
or perhaps three. Or four. Or five. All mortal,
these lovers, mortal men. But only I
was cursed for these lovers, cursed, by those
who merrily danced into
the delightful, welcoming beds
of those who danced with many loves,
and could whisper of the touch of gods.

They claim I cried when my lover, my prince,
first caressed my golden skin. They claim I wept
at the taste of his lips, screamed at the fierce strength
of his bruising arms. Rape, they named it, rape, and cried and cried
for the rape of all Troy's women in revenge, as if
such pain could only be healed
through other women's agony. They claim, they claim,
in songs and songs. Songs they used
to justify their swords,
to justify the fires they themselves would set.

At first, I told him no.
At first.

Men love and love, my mother said,
like gods in their eternal quest
for something changing, something novel
not found in an immortal's arms.

And yet not like gods, for we think we can hold them,
the way we hold water in a cup,
never seeing the cracks and holes
so carefully concealed beneath the glaze.

DIOSCURI

In the dry dust, their names return to me,
    swaddled in silence.

                            Castor. Polydeuces.

        My hands clench, but I can find
        no tears within my eyes.

The tale came upon harsh sandals,
beating upon the dry earth: One brother
dead: the other –

                Not dead

The palace whispered. The horses
trembled at a breath; the trees
flickered at the whispers. *Not dead*,
the palace whispered, *and not alive.*
I saw them watch my golden arms,
the light flickering in my hair,
and saw my sisters, seeing, steal from me,
to hide themselves in mortal shadows.

Night's slim fingers wove the tale,
setting it in heavy shadows: of my divine brother's
final trade, and my mortal brother's final gasp:
and their ending: their untwinned lives,
half held deep within in the corn rich earth,
and half freed in the unsmiling stars,
ever divided, to never die, but never speak

with living human souls, and only to meet
in those rare chanced twilight times
when light and twilight danced with the wind,
and the olive trees shook with the approaching stars,
when twin and twin might brush their hands,
and for a moment remember brotherhood.

My brothers?

Silence. Silence. And sudden weeping.

      Grief came
not as a storm, nor a steady flood,
but as a fox, hidden in green, stalks his prey –
but the slightest of rustles to warn of his approach,
or as a thief, leaving the lightest of footfalls
upon a wooden floor, leaving me
stricken, unsure of what hunted me,
or what, in truth, I had lost.
I did not move. I did not eat.
I was Helen, golden, divine.
And all the world seemed bathed in grey,
and I so distant, distant, from it.

Into the dry river sink
my wingless words,
mingling with ivory dreams.
Perhaps. Or lost –
here in the shadows where all seems lost,
even the dreams and shadows that led me here.

Later they said I stood upon Troy's walls,
and searched for them, my brothers,
knowing nothing of their deaths,
searching for their tents, their banners,
searching for them, my tamers of horses.

But I searched not for both,
but for one, or the other,
for the moment slipped between sun and shadow,
the cloaks of day and robes of night,
the dark earth and dancing stars,
the thin line between life and death,
which they danced upon
as others followed.

PAREGORON

Mother, brothers, sisters, twin –
so filled, so filled, were Sparta's halls.
So empty, so empty, in their absence.

He held me, my lover, my king,
as we raised songs for my brothers, the twins.
He held me, my lover, my king,
as I wept long into the night,
and almost, almost, I forgot
my love, my prince. Almost.

I sat beside a fire when he came,
my love, my king, sword resting lightly in his hands.
Dark words over darker waters.
The father of my mother, the king
dead in Crete. He ran dark fingers
through his hair. *I would not leave you*
in your grief.

        Cold, cold our halls.
        The gold had slipped from bright marble columns,
        stealing with it all warmth.

Though the princes remain
to entertain you.

        Cold, cold, my hands,
        and even the light that poured from them

seemed dimmer, dimmer, in the fading light.

The briefest of touches, of skin upon skin.
The briefest of kisses, lips upon lips.
In the corners, shadows beckoned,
and I thought I heard a goddess' laughter.

In the distance, thunder sounds,
and I shake, I shake, though free of dreams.

That last night I turned to him,
my love, my king, and bathed his body
with my tongue and tears. *They leave soon,
the princes*, he whispered beneath me.
You shall be safe. His tongue danced
in my ear. *Feed me your sweet potions,
and let us dream.* But that
was no night for dreams, and
I did not allow our tongues to rest,
until his absence filled the room.

Bright the shores of Crete,
so bright, bright beneath the moonlight.
Dark, dark, the halls of Sparta,
as I watched the endless dance of stars,
and watched for hopeful shadows.

He came to me then, my prince, my love,
holding my shaking body in his own.
He came to me then, my prince, my love,
and with all else lost, I followed.

BRIBES

He told me nothing of it until we were at sea,
the water spraying upon my face. *My father's brother*,
I thought, I said, not looking at my lover, my prince.
I dangled golden hands in the flowing waves,
as the slaves bent to their oars. *A year*, I said,
though already knowing one year would not
satiate this longing. *One year. No more.* I turned my head
to watch the place where Sparta stood,
could I but see past the edge of the sea.
No more. I shivered beneath his lips.
Far more, he whispered, then caught his lips in mine,
as the sea covered us in its finest foam.

A gift, he whispered, later, as we rocked beneath
a canopy of sheerest silk, watching the shimmering sun.
No, no mere gift. Fate. A bribe. A choice. His hands
twisted, clenched. *Lights dancing in the trees.*
A wealth of laughter. Honeyed voices in the sweetest songs.
And promises, rich promises, in honeyed bronze,
wrapped around my throat. Kingdoms. Wisdom.
Skill at war. I chose –

Water sprayed above us.

His fingers lingered near my throat.

a gift. A gift.

        His fingers tightened near my throat.
        The east wind tugged at my breath.

Not for beauty, though their beauty seared

*my eyes, until I could not bear the sun. Not for wisdom,
though they held insights immortal
and might have told my path. Not for glory,
though my light strained eyes wondered if
I could bring that pain to others. Not for wealth.
I had counted golden coins and felt
their soft and endless chill. For ease.
I chose for ease. I would not rule
three kingdoms, nor be a great warlord,
of wisdom in a battle. I would
not bring my city pain; I would
not let death tiptoe so close
to my wife, my lover, upon her hill,
dancing amidst pink purple flowers.
I chose for ease. Only love
would guide my path. Only love
would enter my city, would darken
my brothers' paths. Only love
and beauty, the beauty granted
by the gods.* He kissed my hair, my golden hair
that had filled the hands of my love, my king.
His lips slid down my neck. I saw
he had clasped my hands within his own.
His hands burned. *The only way
to save my city from certain war.*
His grip tightened, and my bones ached.
*Love. Most beautiful, most beautiful, love.
You would be mine, and so you were,
for a touch of a golden apple.*

    The south wind stole my breath from me.

Since birth I had been no more than
a plaything for gods and men,
a golden toy to be tossed
into a hungry wind. I could not say
why his words ripped at my throat,
why I could no longer see,
why the waters, akin to me,

who would dance beneath my father's rage,
seemed to stretch out their arms to me.

I beg you, hold no anger, he whispered,
letting his tongue linger in my ear. *A gift,*
I said, *and gift you were. And such a gift, such a gift.*
And mine, all mine. The only way
to save my city
from certain war. His fingers lingered
on my skin. The boat swayed gently
in the wind. I could say nothing,
trapped beneath his lips.

I would not believe him. I would not.
I, daughter of thunder, was no mere prize
for a goddess' whim. I would not believe him.
I would not. I had made this choice myself,
and making it, I swallowed all its burning.

The dry dust robs me of my voice,
and each dream I grasp swiftly dissolves
before it becomes a song.

TROY

They never sing, in any tales
of the utter *newness* of doomed Troy, its ascent
a tale still of living memory, though it climbed
on cities shattered long before. No animals
roamed its god wrought streets, so
free of muck and blood. It smelled, it smelled –
of rich perfumes and dark flowers,
so distinct
from the mortal cities I had known.

He sang me down the streets, my prince, my love
and I laughing danced to his drumming voice.
They came, they came, to see the woman,
born of a golden egg, to see their singing prince,
and raised their voices in a dulcet song,
and I laughing heard no bitterness. Sunset
turned the streets to blood. Shadows
rose in darkened alleys.
They danced for me, I thought,
and laughed.

I danced for them, his brothers, the fifty sons
of the aged king, and the other lords –
the cousins, husbands, heroes, hangers-on
who lined the columns of Priam's hall
with their fierce faces and goblets of wine.
I danced.

Let it be said: as I danced, they clapped
and shouted in joy and praise.

Let it be said: as I danced, they wanted
golden Helen, and watched with hunger.
Let it be said: as I danced, they thanked
the gods, and praised Love, pure Love,
for bringing me to their halls to dance.

And after the dance,
they brought me
to the women.

Bone on silver,
silver on bone,
the sound of a harp
the memory of dream.

They greeted me, his sisters, and his brother's wives,
their voices falling from the columns and floors,
as hawks over vermin, as I stood below
searching for faces behind their veils.
Names, so bewildering, so endless. *Andromache.
Creusa. Laodice,* who had known
the son of Theseus. *Polyxena. Nereis,* who stood
with shells woven in her rich hair. *Medesicaste.
Demosthea. Aristodeme. Philomela. Ethionome.*

        And last, a woman
who would not leave the shadows.

You see, said my prince, my love,
I too have a twin. A shadow. His eyes watched the hills.
*She names me cursed. A bringer of fire.
Destroyer of Troy. How I envy you
your sisters.*

        Welcome, sister, said the woman.

> *Too brief this welcome. Too soon
> come the fires.*

May the thunder forgive me. I laughed.

Cassandra, they named her,
twin to my lover, my prince,
plain where he shone.
The taste of gods
hung on her lips,
more bitter than beer.
She danced in shadows,
and clung to fire,
running her hands
through its harsh flames,
avoiding the faintest
touch of the sun.

> *Dance with me
> in the olives, on the roofs,*
> I begged her, once.
> *Dance on the walls
> before the saltswept warriors.
> Hold your arms
> into the sun.*

She showed her teeth,
and danced in the shadows,
hidden beneath the roofs of men,
far from the touch of sun,
singing her visions,
which no one, no one
could believe.

                    I poured
wine laced with honey, and walked to each,
pressing their lips against the silver cup.
And still their teeth stayed tightly closed.

Slowly, I met them, one by one, the princes and lords,
sons of heroes and kings, immortals and shadows.
And Aeneas, in the garden, choosing flowers
for his wife, sister of my prince, my love. Thunder sounded,
and knowledge settled upon me
as a bird returning to its nest.

You are the son of Love, I whispered.

His hands tightened upon his lyre.

So my father claims, though I –
I have felt it not.
But no mortal woman names me
as her son. They say I was found upon a hillside,
tended by nymphs, or inside a cave of monsters.
Or brought by my father in a basket of reeds,
with no woman to follow him. Or the mere son
of a slave. A hundred stories I have heard.
And not all of them name love.

I saw the golden veins beneath his skin,
heard thunder roar in a clear bright sky.

You are the son of Love, I whispered.

And what is she to you?

            Her touch so burning upon my skin I ache I ache –

    My mistress. Though I might – I might –
    name her sister.

I placed one finger upon his arm.

And so I may name you kin.

———⚜———

From the mother of my prince, my love,
no kind word, only the whispered name
of his first wife, the mountain dweller,
who still danced, they said, in her cold spring.
I gave to her a golden smile, and danced, and danced,
and clasped my lover's hand more tightly.

———⚜———

She was heavy with childbearing, this queen,
heavy with the weight of years, of loves both human
and divine, her hands stained dark, dark,
with dye, or so she named the stain.
They say she lay with the archer god,
before he slew her children.
They say she followed her youngest son,
to the cursed courts of other lands.
They say she is now a hungry dog,
trotting at the footsteps of a moon goddess,
always sniffing for her children's blood.

———⚜———

I raise my face, but cannot taste
a single scent upon the wind.
I thirst, I thirst.
Dim the memory of water.
Fierce the memory of blood.

———⚜———

I cannot remember

the first night of nightmares, though they came, they came,
my prince, my love, shaking in the night,
crying of the cold as fires blazed
near our bed, with furs piled high,
I pressed against him.
The hillside, the hillside,
the cold hillside.
So cold, so cold.
My hands stroked, and stroked,
but no touch of mine
could remove that inner chill.

Only later did I hear the tale
in whispered words, fragments dropped
where no prince nor queen might hear,
of a prince torn from his nurse's arms,
left upon a cold hillside. No uncommon tale
for peasants and slaves, but no common one
for princes.

                        No one could tell
how he had survived, though some spoke
of a kindly bear, a gentle wolf
who nursed him near her own small pups,
and others spoke of golden gods, or
shepherdesses lovely enough
to bind spirits to them each night. But all knew
how he had returned, to his sister's screams,
as a water maiden stood by his side. And how
he had strode into the palace
as his sister, his twin cried of fire.

Only later did I hear her words,
whispered to a roaring fire.
What god, what god, would take a child such as this?

What god, what god, would not?
I heard no reply from any god,
only her harsh tears, and the cries of women,
and about us, the falling of roofs and walls.

Heavy, heavy, the air of Troy,
heavy from the songs of crystal voices.

                    A month, a month,
of dancing women and laughing men,
of rich wines and yielding sweets
of a desperate wish for my lover's mouth.
Another month of tumbles in bed,
of laughing with women he had once loved.
A third month of music and of shows,
of watching men play with swords,
and light dance upon their skin.
A fourth month: a long dark cry
and the long ships landing upon the shore.

WAR

Traders, I whispered, though my eyes
could see the glitter of swords and shields
and hear the rasps of arrows. *Traders*.
My prince did not even answer this,
instead swinging upon the walls, to stand
beside his brothers. *Lower the gates*,
Hector called out. Bronze clanging
filled the streets. I threw my hands
over my ears. My new sisters watched me
with contempt, and in the shadows
Cassandra sobbed, then laughed.
A shadowed goddess dropped
scraps of apple upon the ground.

We climbed the walls to watch, my love and I,
the spill of Achaeans upon the shore. No mere raid this.
Even I, untrained in war, could see the tents,
could see the food dragged from the ships,
the tools for twisting metal from fire. We watched.

I once drank from the teats of a bear.
It should have given me courage.

Our hands, met, clasped, came undone.

I hear, I hear the clanging;
I watch dreams falter and break beneath that sound.

It was not endless battle, those ten years,
but close enough: a constant noise
of shields and swords, of arrows and tears,
of frantic songs and love and drink,
a ceaseless stink of burning flesh,
the persistent sweetness of buzzing bees,
and the endless craving for honeyed sweets,
the daring runs through Troy's deep tunnels,
to drag in food and coin.

Beneath my hands, my gardens bloomed
in the darkest nights of war. As my lover slashed
the thighs of men, I bent to my many herbs,
and savored the sweetness of fresh mint. As my love
watched the clanging of the swords, I pulled
fragrant grapes from clinging vines,
and placed them on my lips. Fires might rage
and men cry of swords, but green things grew,
or so I told myself, unheeding the steady retreat
of the forests that once ringed golden Troy.

And the nights! Ah, the nights! Heavy
with the perfumes of flowers and rich wines,
light with fiery laughter and fevered whispers,
where I clung to my love, and he to me,
both of us utterly lost to war.

Come back. Come back.
I cannot breathe.
Come back.

In later years, I wondered: was it
ten years of war, that felt like one,

in all its frantic clanging of spears and shields,
or one year of war, that felt like
ten. They tracked the time, they said,
the priests, watching every journey
of the angry sun, and yet, in later years,
I could never count ten seasons of blood,
but only anguished hours warped
by a single lonely hour,
for time shifts and sways in war,
its beat uncertain, its movement pulsed
by the shattering of arrows and spears
and not the blazing march
of an indifferent sun.

In ten long years upon the shore,
they never built. Their tents remained,
battered by the wind and sea,
sometimes replaced by newer cloth,
and their sand pits moved, pushed by
wind and sea. But no more than that: never
a single shed or stall, never a
high tower with which to watch the sea,
and the storm tossed sea roads leading home.

I drink dust, I drink dust,
beg for death, and suck down sand:
The divine throbs through my blood
and I drink no respite.

PROTOS

The first year: that was the worst,
and yet not the worst. The ships arriving
on our shores; the tents rising upon the sands;
the taunts of the men from our high walls. A glimpse –
no more, but a half seen glimpse –
doubtless a mistake – of my love, my king
hidden in the sand pitched tents.
They will leave, my lover said, unsmiling. *They will
grow hungry, tired of war.* I clung to his arm,
and thought of my love, my king,
but said no other word.

War is not so new a thing,
or so the songs and tales all say. My own city
had known its wars, and so had Troy:
its walls still showed the signs of fire,
and its men drilled with spear and shield
for memory and foresight. Nor did it seem so new
in time, when ears learned its rough rhythms,
when eyes grew dulled to endless wounds,
when dreams filled with ordinary things
mixed with the signs of battle.

But that first battle in all its chaos –
new, so new. So very new.
As new as the sound of rattling chains
raised in the hands of the princes of Troy,
raised as their eyes rested upon me.

The swift curtain dances
between me and death;
I wrap myself in its folds.

The battle still raged when he arrived,
hands heavy with copper and bronze,
groaning at their weight. He dropped
the chains upon the floor, and for a moment
I heard a battle cry
upon the wind,
though within our rooms
we felt no wind.
He knelt, and watched me
with quiet eyes.

    I will not be chained. I paced
    about our room, once so wide and warm,
    now so thin and cold. *I am queen of Sparta,*
    daughter of Zeus. I will not be chained,
    like a bloodied dog untrusted by its lords,
    or some beast dragged here from distant lands.

They know you not.

  Smoke spun shadows
  inside our rooms.

    Have I fled the city walls?

Have you seen your lord and king?

    In that dust and fire, who could name
    one lord from the next?

  He rose, to throw
  another small stick

upon our tiny fire.

And still you name yourself Sparta's queen.

In chains, I am no queen of Troy.

Outside, a battle cry arose,
then halted.

The lambent webs of love
hold my eyes, my skin.
I am trapped, trapped,
and yet I find myself
feeding these webs,
praying for their growth.

To them I went, the princes of Troy,
in the great hall of Priam. Great it was, I thought,
I who had danced with immortals upon the hills,
but had not yet seen the great halls of Egypt.
Nonetheless, I went, bedecked in rich purple,
obtained from some land across the sea,
where men still fought fierce monsters
and left women chained for dragons. My hair
I laced with gold and pearls, and other gems
gleaming in the light of fires. My feet I laced
with silver sandals. My hands I let fill
with golden light. And so I paced
into their halls.

They watched me, Priam's fifty sons,
their eyes heavy with hunger. (Even Hector
of the joyous marriage, even he –
could not remove his eyes from me.) I walked
and let their eyes feast upon my form, and knelt

but briefly before Priam's throne. No more
than a king might offer another king. No less.
I stood, and met his eyes, ruler to ruler,
queen to king.

                I wear no chains.
                I opened my hands.
                Golden light spilled
                upon the polished floor,
                and for a moment,
                Priam's eyes
                gleamed.

Think of how they would shine
upon your skin. A pale tongue
lined his lips. *But my sons,*
oh my sons. Think not that they consider
only your beauty. Think instead upon this:
that they know you brave enough
to leap into the battles below. Unless –
unless something occupied your hands.

        Hungry those eyes.
        So hungry.
        Wet those tongues.
        So wet.

                I wear no chains.

His long fingers gathered
beneath his chin. *Then*
something else must be found
for those golden hands.

        ⁂

They gave me gardens, gardens,
upon the roofs of Troy, ringed by
arrows and spears. Always they watched

as I knelt among my herbs and dirt,
as I coaxed vines from rough planters,
as fruits sprung from my hands.
Never had I been a grower of fruits
or tender of vines, and yet
they grew, fed by love and pain,
or perhaps by my father's rich rains
now draining from my hands.

The wind mocks, and mocks.
I hear the river's distant throb,
and see only dust and sand.

I fed sweet drugs to the princes of Troy,
the sons and daughters of Priam. I fed
sweet drugs to the old men as they perched
atop the walls, watching the seas and the soldiers below,
remembering their own times at the wall. I fed
sweet drugs to the soldiers of Troy. They
smiled at my approach, smiled, smiled,
and I dropped drugs into their water.
Power, power, I thought, and yet,
the walls of Troy held me close.

        Lost, lost,
                all is lost.
I stumble in dreams,
                clutch for gold,
         to find white sand
     draining from my hand.

In the city came the whispers, of how Agamemnon
ripped his daughter from the pale arms
of my sister, my twin. Of how he had placed
the quivering child upon the altar, of how
the knife had gleamed under the moon,
and how none had seen her, after.

My hands fumbled in their weaving,
fumbled upon the lyre's strings. Restless, I walked,
the stones cold, cold, upon my feet,
and yet not cold enough.

The fires dwindled to sullen coals.
My lover held me in his arms,
and we dared not think of children.

Tightening, tightening, those webs of love.
So sweet, so sweet, this pain.

He was wounded in that first year,
my lover, my prince. A wound
like an earthquake on a dark night,
waking all from uneasy dreams. I had thought him
held by armor. Safe. Invincible.
Forgetting that even the immortal gods
may be wounded, may drip rich ichor
into their mother earth, birthing fair flowers in their pain.
Forgetting he had no sea mother
to dip him into darker seas.

No flowers leapt from his wound. Only dripping blood,
slow and steady, from the smallest of holes
in his shoulder. Smaller wounds
have opened doors for death.
He laughed.

I dragged him to the springs, first the hot,
then the cold, washing the blood from his armor
and body. About me other women stood,
washing the bodies of their own lovers
and lords, their arms heavy with wounds
and soiled cloth. We washed, and watched
the blood flow down towards the river,
and spared no thought for the Achaean horses,
who soon would be sipping
from that bloodied stream.

Tightly I pulled linens about his arm. Softly I murmured
my mother's spells, and called the thunder
to be his shield. The earth trembled as I prayed.
So gentle our love that night. So rough. So fierce.
Though no touch of skin or lips
could veil the sound of Cassandra, weeping.

DEUTEROS

The second year: that was the worst,
and yet not the worst. They would not leave
our shores, the ships; they would not cease
their angry drumming on their shields.
The clanging throbbed upon my skin. I seized
my love, my prince, and let the pounding
move between us, let the cries of war
bind our hearts to a single beat.

A harp of bone and copper in my hands.
A cry of the wind.
My fingers tremble upon the strings.
Somewhere, I hear a river sing.

About the city
villages emptied, their buildings soon standing
bare to wind and sun, soon to crumble
beneath raids and rain, with only ghosts
to mourn the falling walls. And below us,
a city grew, of tents and ships,
bonfires and pits. From the shores
their cries rang out, the crash of metal,
the tumult of voices. And sometimes
as the gentle evening fell, chased
by wind and rain and night, it came:
the calm of laughter and song,
a fall breeze in a summer heat,
and for a moment we could almost forget

that they had come to us in war.

      They are no more
than raiders, said the exhausted Antiphonus.
*Famed for cattle raiding, but no more. They cannot
take much more than this. Their men
will sail their thousand ships
back into the sea, leaving us here
in the quiet shadow of these rough mountains.
They sing tales of their raiding, their kills
not of long waits beneath stone walls.
They will not last. They will not.*
The fires flickered at his words,
and a goddess laughed faintly
in the dancing shadows.
My prince, my love, ran his fingers over his lyre,
and Aeneas, wise Aeneas, and foresighted Helenus,
and Hector, tamer of horses, said nothing.

They watched me without end, the princes,
their eyes shining in the dark, their hands
never far from their sharp bronze knives.
They watched, and whispered, and followed my steps,
whenever I moved from my lover, my prince. They watched.
Not my beauty, though that snared the eyes of others,
not my dancing, though even women smiled.
They watched, and kept me behind their gates,
and said nothing of my words of love.

Ghosts chase me. I would sleep,
but their cool hands reach for my eyes,
and beneath these hands, I cannot rest.

They gave to me the city roofs, and so I raised
great pots of earth, enriched with honeyed tears,
molded by my own golden hands, and planted
the seeds I had taken from fair Sparta,
from my mother's quiet chambers. Vines rich
with fruit, and golden corn, those too
I grew, but my heart was given to my herbs,
and the sweet potions I brewed from them.

Many, many came seeking to forget,
with something graver and darker than wine.
Others came in search of sleep,
or to soothe the wild thumpings
that overtook their ragged hearts.
Others came for courage, or an end to pain,
and still others came for healing.

And so I soothed the city with my herbs.
Magic, some named it, though it was rarely that,
merely knowledge and study, the wisdom of years,
the growing of plants. And if some dreamed visions,
and spoke to gods, or held maidens of air
tightly to their chests, who could say
if this was a trick of immortals, or merely
the brewing of herbs, of power?

You give false hope, my unsister said
watching me from beneath the shadows,
evading the lightest touch of sun or light.
And even falser dreams.
Before them lies only fire and war,
slavery and death. Not the peace or joy
promised by your herbs, or the glorious embrace
of laughing gods, who say slick lies
from thicker lips. I could not see
her face. *You give false hope.*

> *Or respite.*

What is the difference,
in the shadows?
What is the difference,
in death?

The cold dark stones beneath my feet.
The water that was not water.
The grass that was not grass.
The shadows, the shadows,
moving through the water that was not water.

You will know, I said.
Prophecy came uneasy
to my tongue. My throat was thick
with words. *You will know, you will know.*
Here. I have potions
that will help you sleep.

She once sang, you know, Aeneas said,
nodding towards my unsister, my prince's twin.
And played the lyre, as if Orpheus himself
had trained her fingers.

> My fingers slid over
> my ashen harp.

Almost I thought of wedding her, then,
to wed a voice that made
the very rafters tremble, to wed
a lyre that made the very birds cry.
He smiled. *You think me a poor poet,*
perhaps.

But it matters not. She sought
the arts of prophecy, and I –

well, I, unseeking, have sought
the arts of war.

Outside the walls, thunder rolled,
and men beat upon narrow drums,
letting the beat roll across
the roiling seas and quiet shore.

> Inside the walls,
> my unsister drew rich veils
> about her face, and retreated
> into darker halls.

> *I do not know who time might name*
> *the greater artist.*

I had laughed with the lovers of my lover, my king,
had known of the lovers of Theseus. And yet
the thought of the first wife of my prince, my love,
made my guts sicken and burn. The mere sound
of her radiant name, and the world lurched
beneath my feet, and nearby walls
provided little aid.

And so his sisters told me of her.

Lovely, lovely, an immortal naiad –
whose form shifted like the spring
her home, her laughter the sweet fall of water
upon dry and thirsty skin. Lovely, lovely.
He had been lost, my prince, lost
in the trees that ringed her spring,
lost, lost in her arms.

I too had had other lovers, other loves. I too
recalled the taste of my lover, my king.
I too remembered that he waited nearby,

ringed by his men. And I remembered
the coolness of a spring, the comfort of shadows,
and shook when I saw the eyes of my prince, my love,
shift to the hills of her home.

And this too, they whispered,
that Love herself had bent to his lips,
running her fingers through his hair.
A sight I saw in night's dark hours,
when my love, my prince, lay elsewhere,
and Love changed me into fire and stone,
trapped in the ice of night.

I would not think of this. I would not.
And yet I did. Golden laughter
rang, faint as distant trumpets
calling warriors to arms, and I longed,
I longed, for water.

I stand on sands that are not sands,
play a harp that is no harp,
and feel a wind that is not wind.

If you question my tale, if you question me:
if you question why I would remain
hidden behind walls of mud and stone
resting in gardens and couches of silk,
as harpers and drummers played at nightly feasts,
as the city wearily buried its dead, and pondered
every scrap of grain and strip of meat,
remember the world that held me close,
that held me in its torturous dance:
a world of immortal whims, and more:

a world where women could be
no more than prizes at a funeral game
though valued more than two gold coins
a world where our worth could be measured
in oxen, and where when asked to choose between a woman and a cow,
a man might well choose the cow.

     I drove a city
mad for love. And still I stumble,
whimpering, wondering how I might
bind love with my golden hands,
the same hands that helped drive
that city mad.

Inevitable, I suppose, that my love, my prince,
would watch my steps, my words, for any hint
that I might be as untrue to him,
as I had been to my lover, my king. I could
bathe his foot with my tongue, slide golden fingers
down his bronzed skin, suck the honey
from his lips, and still he would hear
woman, woman. Divine, golden –
still mortal. Still woman. Watch. Listen
to her dreams. Her lover stands
outside these walls. He waits. He watches.
He loves. And I, in seeing, grew in fear,
still knowing, still *seeing*, his other loves:
the water nymph, dancing in the trees,
Love herself, brilliant and cruel.
And so, inside the topless walls of Troy,
we built our own small walls,
though behind our walls, our love still grew,
ever more desperate and strong,
swelling with each despairing touch.

TRITOS

The third year: that was the worst,
and yet not the worst. Food grew scarce.
My vines wilted in the heat. We longed
for bloody meat, for fresh gathered figs,
to wander again through darkened forests,
and hear the voices of lesser gods,
even as the great gods fingered our heated courts
and our walls trembled at their passing.

They dreamed visions, these princes,
and sang their dreams: Helenus,
with his long unshadowed sight,
Aesacus, singer of doom,
Laocoon, handler of snakes, singer to dragons,
and watched the flights of birds
and the dance of dreams, learning but this:
no vision, no dream, held the strength
to stop the coming of doom.

As the war progressed, they sometimes locked
Cassandra in a room, whispering the tale
of how she had refused the very lord of light,
the lord of truth and healing, who could command
the very chariot of the sun, of how she had denied
him entrance to her bed, and turned
the sweetness of her lips from his.
He would take no mortal by divine force, they said,
and so with a single caress of heated skin,

had let her see the future. Madness.

Lies, all lies, Cassandra told us,
from her corner wreathed in shadows.
(He was fond of her, my lover, my prince,
and so she came to our chambers after
night wrapped the city in her cloak,
to huddle in a corner and tell her tales.)
No god touched me. It was a man.

       Sister. Sister. You cannot –

*A man. In this world where mortal women
drink the kisses of gods, I know –
what touched me, took me, was a man.
What bruised my arms and legs was a man.
I called to gods, and heard but silence.
He may well have blamed his god,
may well have cursed me in that name,
and yes, I heard his voice cry out
the name of his god as he seized my hair.
But he was all too mortal in his rage.
And all too mortal in his rape.*

                    For a moment, I remembered –

      A lie, the prince, my lover, whispered,
      enfolding me in his arms. *And that the true tragedy
      of her tale: she cannot even remember it, to tell.*

I was but eight, she whispered.
Eight.

She pulled a veil about her face,
and stepped back into the shadows.

        ⁓

The sun, she once told me,

burned to bone and truth,
showing mercy to none.
And so she hid in shadows, fearing
even the smallest touch of light,
sleeping behind the safety of curtains,
emerging to gaze upon the stars,
before hiding in her shadows, and spoke
of the shadows that danced before her eyes,
of unsought days and unseen years. But who could
believe such shadowed tales, here
in the sturdy city of Troy,
guarded by such stately towers?

I remember. I remember
the women. Weaving in the great rooms,
singing in the great hall, carrying water and herbs
to cure the men. Women practicing with bow and knife,
and raising angry spears, joining the men
upon their raids on Achaean camps.
(Do not imagine this a war
only of men. Women too could shake bright spears;
women too could die on knives.)
I remember. I remember.

The clank of chains
echoes in my ear.
I stir, I stir,
and still the chains sound.
Still the chains sound.

Sometimes we stood upon the walls, we women,
to watch the Achaean men in their endless sport,
or watch a skirmish or fleeting raid,

or learn something of the arts of war.
And so it was that a lord or two
might see a daughter of Troy, and feel
the touch of the goddess who imprisoned me.
And so it was that Achilles looked with bright hunger
upon Polyxena, sister of my lover, my prince.

She had been kind to me, that unsister,
showing me her bright embroidered silks,
her swiftest weavings, her brightest songs,
as she fiercely gripped her well crafted knife.
A match, indeed, for Achilles, in all his deadly wrath,
had the Fates allowed it, or had they met
outside the bounds of war.

He took another, a young slave,
to partner him in his shoreside tents.
She took no one, but watched him from the walls.

>   And in the end, perhaps, they met,
>   shadow to shadow, shade to shade,
>   as she pulled her garments closely about her,
>   as his son slew her upon his tomb.

Something breaks beneath my feet.
Bone, perhaps. Or dreams.

They took other women, the Achaeans, women who came
by cart and path carrying goods for comfort and trade,
women who ventured from our walls for flowers
and grain, women who came to find the bodies
of their lovers and lords, snatched to serve in seaside tents.
Women who sailed upon the seas,
coming to that shore for water, and women who
did not sail at all, but were pulled

from unguarded cities and broken homes.
And I, unstolen, untaken, remained
encased in silk and love, safe behind
the muddy walls and rough dressed stones
of the topless towers of Troy.

They say in Troy I named myself
abhorred and sinful, no fit wife
to my prince, nor fit sister
to my kin. They say I named myself
a horrible conniving bitch.
In this, I assure you,
they lied.

                I may have felt
the mark of sin. But never did
I name it aloud, or give myself
that name. I was shackled, fettered
to love, and that was name enough.

Always, always the fear that he would be stolen,
taken to some rich enchanted isle,
there to half forget the mortal lands,
to forget all mortal women – No. I was Helen.
I would not let him forget, nor let him be taken.

Again she left her locked room, to wander
among the shadows of our halls, and came to me
as I wove cloaks for my love, my prince,
and hangings to fight the frequent chills.
They name you daughter of Nemesis,
my unsister whispered, clutching the marble column
as if its chill could fortify her bones.

*And that you come here
as revenge against us all.*

> It was a tale
> I had not heard. *My mother walked
> on mortal stones,* my voice said,
> as my mind whispered
> *Castor, twisted upon a spear;
> Pollux, dancing in shadows;
> Philonoe, lost to trees.*
> My fingers tingled in remembered pain.
> *Retribution drinks deeply
> from my skin.*

She touched
my face. *Doubtless why
she walks, with fire,
upon your heels.*

> Almost, almost, I turned
> to look.

TETARTOS

The fourth year: that was the worst,
and yet not the worst: almost I failed to see
the hulking soldiers on the golden sands,
their shouts of war and tiny fires,
the arrows that fell upon our streets,
so much had these become the daily parts of life,
as ordinary as eating bread,
or the errands of a daily life,
a river burning with the wrath of gods.

Always, we searched for the signs of gods:
the cries of herons, the flights of eagles,
the falling of leaves, the rising of smoke.
We watched for the immortals in the clang of battle,
for the light that signaled their fingers,
for the robes of laughing Eris, her fingers
laced in blood, hanging on the shields of War.
Mortal, half mortal, all watched the signs:
and half mortal, immortal, all wondered
how to move the mighty thunder.

We cast lots, we cast lots,
desperate to hear the words of gods,
to know if we would die or live,
drink our fill of rich red wines,
die beneath a lover's rich kiss
or die beneath a cold bronze spear.
We watched smoke, watched smoke,
desperate for a single sign,
to tell us if we should plant our seeds,

or creep through the tunnels,
darting between the soldier tents
to find another rocky land.
We drew blood, we drew blood,
and waited at the stony places of the gods
to hear nothing more than silence.

And yet. And yet. Away from those stones,
from those tombs, echoes of whispers
filled my ears; tingles of *other*
filled my hands. I saw shadows dart
from house to house, and road to road,
and my throat filled with the songs of gods,
but when I opened my mouth,
I found only silence on my tongue.

See the dull jewels at my throat,
the dimmed rubies and faded sapphires.
Thirst steals gold from my hands,
and I have no dreams to fill them.

How could the immortals not join that war
when their children filled the ranks of the armies,
and their daughters came to tumble in warrior beds?
Every immortal had a child there, it seemed,
or some man given divine favor, a touch of light,
shimmering through the skin, a false hope
of strength. Or a lover, or a wanted lover,
someone to tumble for a night, to know, to taste
the desperation of mortal blood.

They blamed me, and cursed the gods
for the long years of war. The very gods

that shook the earth, that bent
the very winds to their commands,
the very gods who had caused my birth,
and me, trapped behind the walls,
lost in herbs and weaving.

I dreamed of her, that gentle nymph,
singing gently near her forest spring,
her face all sweetness, her slender hands
clawing at me with the talons of hawks.

In my gardens, his mother and I
harvested leaves for bitter drinks
that might halt the screaming of the men.
I thought of my prince, my love, of how
his lips had lingered at my throat.

Do you truly know
what you hold in your arms each night?
A child of fire, a burner of walls.

                      I thought of his fire
                      against my lips.

a man who sucked at the teats of bears,
And gained nothing from it but weak milk.
A man with no more concern for us,
than a mountain shrieking its divine defiance
with molten fire and heavy ash
to the villages at its feet.

Her eyes stayed dark beneath her hood.

                Perhaps, I answered, *he might*
                have had more thought for Troy,

> *had you not left him on a barren hillside.*

I said nothing to the prince, my lover,
but still he shook, he shook. *The hillside,*
he whispered, *the barren hillside, the cold the cold*
the crying of goats I hear it I hear it I hear it still
it never leaves the crying of goats always
the night always the hunger always the cries
for milk for water for something to hold
against the wind the crying the crying
the crying tell me a tale
a tale a tale

                      And holding him against the fire,
                      I did.

We went to hell, my twin and I,
or at least its mouthpiece. *You cannot die,*
she said to me. Golden light poured
over my hands. I looked into
the cobalt skies, searching
for a hint of rain. *You enter.*
It seemed a simple place,
a dry well formed of rocks and clay,
with nothing below but darkness.
I will hold the rope. Ants crawled
along the stones. I swung
my legs into the darkness, and allowed
my sister to lower me into hell.

Hell *hissed.*

I nearly screamed, but the laughter of
my sister, my twin, hovered above,
and so I descended into hell.

Long that journey, or so it seemed

as she lowered the rope, and I felt
the walls of that dry well.
Leave nothing in hell, so the tales said,
but a single touch upon those walls
stole my blood and skin.
You cannot die, although the gods themselves
could be trapped in hell's swift mists.
You cannot die. Heroes and singers
had returned, with nothing more
than a grey cloud about their faces.
You cannot die. I left more blood
upon the walls, and as I did,
hell *sang*.

        Sang? My lover ran light fingers
        over my skin. *We sing at death*
        as flames consume us. I had not thought
        to hear hell sing.

            It was but a moment.

        Sometimes, we need but a moment
        to die.

A chill seized my fingers
at the song, and I released
the rope, and tumbled down
into the darkness, until my golden feet
touched the floors of hell. And at my touch
only silence, silence, and a whisper
that might have been a wind.

        Dark, and undark,
            the edges of hell,
                before the crossing of the dry river,
                    before the passage through the gates.

        Gone, gone, the rope that had held me
            to the mortal world above.

Waiting for me upon the stones
that were not stones, by the gates that were not gates,
that might have been formed from ivory and horn,
or might have been formed from more human cores,
or from nothing at all, a crone, or not a crone:
an elderly man, or a young girl, fresh
as an apple licked by a goddess. The wind
that was not a wind chafed my eyes. I looked
at my arms, once golden, now grey, pale grey,
and even that uncolor fading into nothing. The crone
threw back her head, and I heard laughter
that was not laughter.

Swan girl.

It was neither hot nor cold, but cool –
cool with a wind that was not wind. The stones
that were not stones
felt rough upon my pale grey feet.

Swan girl.

        Above me, I heard a cry,
        the voice of my sister, my mortal twin,
        lost in the wind that was not wind.

Swan girl, the crone said, or sung.

        No.

I knew little, but enough to know
I was no swan. I could not soar
above the earth, nestled in a wind
to sail to other lands, no swan
to float upon a tranquil lake
watching my reflection. No swan
to release white feathers in my wake,
to seduce young maidens

with a lift of my beak.

> *No.*

No swan,
the guardian agreed. *No swan,*
perhaps. But swan girl you are.
Flight shines through you.
My feet felt heavy on the unstones.
No mere mortal are you, though you may die.
And this is not your place.

> *They say I cannot die.*

She says you cannot die.

> Her voice, her voice, daring me to taste
> the waters of death. Her cry, her cry,
> of terror, of love, now filling that dry well
> with its dark echo.

And even gods can die. My own cold mistress
dies each year, leaving her blood upon the earth
to stain the autumn leaves.

> Thunder pounding in my head
> that was not thunder, only its distant echo
> robbed of power, robbed of its companion fire.

> *Though it is true:*
your sister, your twin, may cross the dry river
when you may not, may stand upon its dark ferry,
when Charon refuses you passage, may dance
in Elysian when you are no more than mortal bones
clawing at the dirt above, when all your gold
has bled from your pulsing skin. Lonely, lonely,
shall you be, daughter of thunder, daughter of swans,
and well may you long for death. For flight.

The wind that was not wind
bent around me. A cold that was not cold
settled deep within my bones.

> *I am Helen. Helen.*
> *I do not fear.*
> I brought my hands to my face,
> and I feared, I feared.

> *Then how may I die?*

> Another cry, of terror, perhaps,
> or sisterhood. Perhaps. Perhaps.

She might have smiled,
an unsmile, as unreal as the river that was not water
that flowed behind her, beyond the gates that were not gates.
The ferryman grinned, and stretched out his hand,
though my own hands were freed, for once, from gold.

Almost I would that you could grow
the feathers of a swan. Almost.
No, for you to die, some harder task:
before you may die, and join your mortal kin,
first you must learn to sing.

> The brush of feathers against my throat.
> The memory of song.

> *I cannot sing.*

So says a swan
until the end.
And I say again: to embrace your death,
unfeathered child of thunder's rage,
first you must learn to sing.

Sing for me, my lover whispered.
Sing.

    You would have me die?

I would have you with me.

The thought made me warm and sick at once.
The ground trembled beneath me.
His touch so light, so light,
like the feathers of a swan.

    Sing.

I had imagined the song, the cry
that death, that hell had made
as I fell into its mouth. Above, my sister,
my twin, pulled at the rope, her mortal life
clinging tightly to its roughened fibers.
All a dream, all a dream,
caused by nothing more than a sudden fright.
And yet, I could still remember the chill of hell,
and I could sing no more than could
a living swan longing for a mate.

Wingless, these words, wingless,
sinking into the heavy mud
here by the river,
the dry river.

Turn not to me for understanding
of the gods. Though I hold their blood,
and have seen them in the shadows of my eyes,

and felt the richness of their touch,
the madness of their desires,
I know them not, the immortals,
I know them not, though they know me,
and so often have graced me with their touch.

No more understanding than any have
when the earth shifts beneath them,
and all that seemed solid is not.

PEMPTOS

The fifth year: that was the best,
and yet not the best. I hardly needed
to ask his thoughts, my love, my prince,
and he knew mine, flooding across my skin.
Love flowed between us, a placid river
ever ready to escape its banks
and drown those standing on its shores.

ECTOS

The sixth year: that was the worst,
and yet not the worst. My vines
burst in flowers and fruits; my own feet
danced upon the grapes for wine.
We wove endless robes of silk,
and played music against the ceaseless winds.
Daring, I ventured through the dusty tunnels,
letting spiders dance within my golden hair,
daring all for one brief taste of wild trees,
for one swift taste of the forest fountain.

In the shadows, I remember.
I weep without tears,
and remember.

In that sixth year, I slipped outside
the walls of Troy. My gardens could
not hold my skin. I needed air, and trees,
the touch of wind. Always the wind in Troy
felt caught in dust, always the wind
felt trapped by the walls of men.

(They, too, were brothers, cousins, my blood remembered,
although to me the wind upon my cheek
was no more than swiftly moving air.)

I changed into a woolen gown. This
was no journey for linens and silks. My hair

I covered with a woolen hood, that it might
not be seen in the golden sun, that men
might think me no more than a slave.

And garbed, I entered those cool tunnels
carved by children and men, that with
their dust and mud opened the city
to endless life. Empty that day, empty.
Beyond the tunnels, Achaean raiders roamed,
and no mother would lose a child
for the mere hope of food and trade.

Dust covered my golden hands when I emerged.
I raced from the tunnel to the green gold woods,
my eyes set upon the trees. If an arrow flew at me,
I did not hear, and did not see:
my eyes were trapped in the green sea
that pulled at me, pulled at me.

Never had I been one for forests,
for all my playing in the woods. I had chosen
stones and mud and silk and fire,
and yet the trees welcomed me,
bending their branches from my path,
to let me enter cleanly, closing behind
to shape walls behind my back.
Daughter of Zeus, I thought, and nodded in thanks
before breathing, breathing, the air of the trees.

Hardly did I know my path. I touched rough bark,
felt dead leaves against my skin, even as my eyes
drowned in green. I heard the singing of a spring,
one clear song raised where Earth could not restrain
the joy of dance from deepest earth. I wandered,
wandered, feeling the deepening of thirst,
and almost raised my voice to answer.

Almost.

       No need to kill this joy with harshness.
I let the spring sing alone, and let its song
draw me near.

I drink from the dry river,
and find no relief.
I feast on shadows,
and I hunger, hunger.

I do not know
if I knew, if I knew.

The spring sang, it sang,
and I thirsted, I thirsted.

A water nymph played in the spring,
taking his feet into her mouth and hair.
My king, my love. His bronze skin
gleamed in the sun. I sank to my knees.
A splash of water. He turned his head.
Not a smile at first. Not then.

A dream.

The naiad's watery form rose and spun, sending
rainbows from her watery hands,
and sweet fountains from her hair.

                 A dream, I agreed.

No maiden, this naiad, but a full grown man,
with a rich beard of water –

A dream.

You are behind the city walls, they say.
Or taken elsewhere. I have not seen —

The maiden-man of water laughed, and laughed,
head swelling in the growing spring.

I have not seen. A dream.

A dream.

Slowly I stepped towards that spinning spring,
my eyes filling with water and shadows.

So long have I have longed
for your return.
So long have I watched the walls,
watched the women who watch the war,
and wondered, and wondered, if your eyes have seen,
or if all is clouded by a cloud of dust.
So long. So long. So long.

A dream.

Lips met, parted, met again. So real the taste.
Water held us both. I caught
his hand in mine. So real the skin.
So firm his legs against my own.

        So clear the sight
        of my lover, my prince.
        So clear the sight
        of the towers of Troy
        ablaze, ablaze
        in the setting sun.

A swirl of water, a shaking of trees,
and he was gone. The spring stood silent,

all water gone, and the trees
utterly still. A trick of a goddesses,
of gods. The spring stank of green decay.
I had dreamed it, I had. Only I knew
I had not.

For six years, only those words:
only those whispered words of dreams.
So long. So long. So long.

Golden light twisted in my hands, my hands.
A dream. A dream. I kissed my lover, my prince,
and drew silken veils about us,
to hide us from mortals, if not from gods,
and dreamed of gardens. And water.

I have loved,
oh how I have loved.
The mountains shudder
before the
strength of my love.
The hawks
shriek with its fury.

Almost I envy you, Creusa said,
joining me upon the walls as I watched the tents.
Almost.

Indeed?

*Not for your beauty, though some
might indeed envy that. But I cannot envy
the hungry glances, the endless eyes. Knowing*

that your lovers might see no more beyond
your near immortal face and skin,
the golden light pouring from your hands.

> I clenched my hands, still filled with dirt
> from my work within the gardens.

No, for that you have not my envy. But for that –

> Beneath our eyes, the armies taunted
> tired war cries. It was no day
> for true battle, nor even a small skirmish,
> but a day of taunts. Of delay.

They will always say that you have known Love.
That you have been her prisoner. Her slave.

> You are wed to the son of Love.

And little love has that brought us.

> The men pounded upon their shields.

I make no claims as does my sister, your lover's twin.
I have no gift of foresight. And yet –
I have seen her, in my dreams. A woman of fire.
A ruler of a city. And another to follow.
And I not by his side.

> Not all dreams dream true.

These are dreams of ivory and gold.
The goddess laughs her golden laugh.
Even ever-young Dawn, they say,
has known the aging of love.

> Upon the field, the signs of Sparta,
> glittering upon shields of bronze.

I would that we were friends.

Or sisters.

The men pounded upon their shields,
and our hands laced together as one.

EBDOMOS

The seventh year. That was the worst –
and yet not the worst. A year of dust,
of warcries and screams,
of petty fights, and prayers for rain,
and silence from the gods. The divine
stirred dimly in my veins. If I were love,
if I were revenge, surely I could end this drought:
surely I could transform dust
into something *other*, something *more*.
But I was only woman, dancing,
kneeling in my garden, sobbing.

The battle ebbed, and the hollow ships
trembled upon the shore. The breath of gods
teased our skins. Arrows hung upon oiled strings.

Too brief, too brief, the pause. Too loud, too loud,
the song of arrows in the endless wind.

I sink, I sink, beneath the touch of Love
and cry out with the pain.
I sink, I sink, feeling her fetters harsh against my skin,
but do nothing to remove them.

Too many within and without the walls of Troy
could name me kin: half brothers, cousins, kin

their veins throbbing with the same immortal blood
that sent golden light flowing over my skin.
Some were women, famed for beauty and grace,
and others men: fierce warriors
who sang with the force of thunder,
who let lightning crackle along their skin.
I watched them dance with mortal lords,
watched them battle with lesser men,
and shivered in the rain. *Brothers, kinsmen*,
but they would not hear, or if they did
would only blame me for their ceaseless wounding.

The sons of thunder strode the field of battle,
laughing below their divine brethren.
The daughters of thunder watched above,
hiding their beauty behind shining clouds.
And I, I alone of thunder's daughters,
sank my feet into mortal earth.

The mother of my lover, my prince, spoke of it,
of her dalliance with a god, of how
she had stepped upon a muddy shore
and felt the god creep upon her legs,
of how she had sunk sobbing beneath the waves,
wrapped within its joy. Even Cassandra
spoke of it, of the god's most deadly sweetness,
of the touch she had flinched from in despair,
after that first more mortal man.
The other princesses spoke of the touch of wind,
the flicker of a candle, the knowing that
other held them, if for but a moment.
Even the slave maids spoke of it,
of bending into the deepest wells,
and hearing the songs of gods,
the whispered touch of something *more*.

But never I. I alone could not speak

of the caresses of the gods,
of the sweetness of their lips.
I gave my lips to mortal men,
and for this they named me divine.

In that seventh year, he left –
if only for a day, a week, a turning of the moon.
What mattered the time? He left,
and I felt each moment stretch, as time
shifts from hour to hour, day by day
never proceeding at the steady pace
the horses of the sun might choose.
He left.

He returned to find me weeping,
huddled under silken cloths. He said no word
as my body rocked, dry of tears
yet not of sobs. He knelt.
Tell me you did not leave, I said, clutching
his arm. *Tell me you would not leave. You are
my air, my sun; without you
I sink far beneath the dark earth,
and cannot move.* He leaned
against our olive bed,
and shut his eyes.

> *If you cling to me,*
> *you will be lost.*

> But with you, I was found.

> *Do not deceive yourself,*
> *my love. Do not think*
> *to find yourself in me.*

I have loved, I have loved,
oh how I have loved.

I would never anger him, I swore.
And yet I did, again, and again.
So worthless the vows we swear in love.
So deeper, more binding, than many more.

Bitter, bitter you may name me,
as I stand upon these grey shores,
the unsand harsh beneath my skin,
and remember, remember
the distant joy of laughter.

Troubles in love? The silver voice of Creusa, she who
caressed the very son of Love,
in her bed each dark night.

> *They say the gods have
> a myriad myriad words for love,
> and none mean well for mortals.*

*Fortunate you are not
mortal then.*

> I picked up a dagger,
> pierced my finger,
> raised my finger to the light.
>
> *Am I not?*

*Immortals, too,
may shed blood.*

> The shock of thunder,
> the cry of a hawk,
> and golden light pulsing from my hands.

We watched for quarrels
among the Achaeans, for any sign
that they might weaken and splinter
upon the shores. And indeed they fought
endlessly beside their fires, their booming voices
sailing above our city walls
to trouble our meals and sleep.
And sometimes, indeed, a ship would depart
swiftly swallowed by a grey horizon
and breaths felt loosened by the sight.
And always, always, the ship would return,
as Cassandra smiled her sad knowledge.

OGDOOS

The eighth year: that was the worst,
and yet not the worst. A year of endless, choking dust,
of failing fountains, of empty wells,
of Troilus gasping at the forest fountain,
the sword of Achilles through his throat,
as by him crept the children of Troy,
fetching sweet water for soldiers with
throats too dry to swallow.

The names of the fallen rang in the songs
of poets and singers, strolling the halls
with their endless chants. *We must not forget*,
and I did not, and yet I did: their names
grew heavy in my mind, too many, too many,
until all that remained was the memories
of shadows and blood, fire and ash,
the scent of the dead, and nameless bones
upon the beach below
the broken city gates,
soon to be covered by wind and sand.

A day of battle; the city cried
in joy and triumph. A god smiled,
and moved a hand. A day of battle;
the city cried, fierce tears that lacked
a taste of joy, or triumph.

Move through life,
the way your fingers would dance upon a flute,
drawing out every note of song.

Meet death in fear, in laughter, in resignation:
meet it knowing you have heard each note.

Not all the heroes at and on the walls
were men. Women came too, gripping
shields and swords, bows and slings,
ready to feel the wrath of war
leaping through their blood. They came in tribes,
on dancing horses, on war chariots
of glistening bronze. They came on foot.
They came by sea. They came alone,
They came, they said, to die near me.

Even I, thunder's child, born of storm and swan,
lover of prince and king, had never seized my destiny
as these women seized their weapons and cried their dooms
into the unconquered sun.

I kept my own bronze knife well sharpened,
its curved edge meant to stroke a human neck
with one quick thrust; its slender point
meant to enter the ribs with no more force
than a lilting song must take
to enter a heart with cheer. I kept it
on my hip, well bound
with a belt of silver and silk. I kept it
at my hand, its jeweled handle
a harsh reminder of my strength.

I had my mother's tricks, the ones
of drugs and thread and loom. And I stroked my knife.
And called that destiny and doom.

———⚜———

A spring. The prince named me friend
and avoided my every move, as I watched
his every step, the goddess pressing upon my throat.
And not just the goddess. His absence
seemed a knife across my throat
stopping my breath,
 a thought that I could not control.
Mind and dreams filled with him;
waking mind thought of little other.
The goddess cradled me in her arms,
as my breath grew ragged, ragged.

He knew, as I knew, all the tales.
He sang, as I could not, all the songs.
He knew, for who did not, that Love herself
had left crafts and fire to nestle
in the arms of war. And no song sang
that she would never return.

Dark, dark the shadows between us.
And in their endless shifting, I could not tell
what mind ruled their movements.

———⚜———

How can any regret love?
Or not regret its passing?

———⚜———

She waited in the shadow of my olive trees,
unsister, untwin, body shaking. In the shadow,
our eyes met, and for a moment, I left my herbs,
to extend a golden hand.

You shake.

Before this war ends, a Danaan will rape me,
as about us his warriors watch and cheer.
When this war ends, a Danaan will take me,
and convey me across the wine-dark seas.
to enter the household of your sister, your twin.
I have seen it in the grey sands of the shore.
I have seen it in the churning of the sea.

                        Theseus's rough hands
            brushed across my skin.

              They will not rape
women royal, women who might claim
descent from a god. Sisters of princes,
daughters of kings. The women of the city –
Bruises, bruises, upon my golden skin,
I, untouchable daughter of thunder.
You, at least, are safe from that. As for
my sister, my twin – I let golden laughter
leave my lips, and tumble into the air,
still heavy with Trojan songs. *More likely*
my cousin. More likely the trickster,
with your gift for tales.

Believe what you wish, unsister, untwin.
And she retreated again into shadow.

Again and again, Apollo seized the arrows of plague,
sending Achaeans and Trojans alike plunging into disease,
bodies wracked with fever and sores. *An insult to the gods,*
some would cry. *Priestesses stolen, raped; sacrifices*
forgotten, hymms unsung. In the seashore camps,
they traded women in blame; in our city they raised fire and smoke,
and let the city temples fill with blood and gold.
A daughter returned, the plague might lift;
a prize of a woman stolen, the battle might rage more deeply.

And all loudly or softly blamed the immortal gods,
who with one bright arrow so carelessly sent
could send a camp to raving fevers.
And none blamed the very act of war,
the siege that kept us trapped behind our walls,
that kept them in their tents beside the sea.
In this it was easier to blame the gods,
easier to blame than mortal folly.

I step into the river, the dry river,
and gather shadows about me.
The harp of copper and bone trembles in the wind,
and almost I hear a song.

    When Apollo's arrows fell
upon the shoreline ships and tents,
we knew. We heard the lingering cries,
the low moans of Achaeans dying, the weeping
of the women who tended them,
the moan of the sea never quite
hiding their cries. My hands shook
over my vines, my herbs,
my sweet drugs that could
combat a wrathful god;
but trapped behind Troy's high walls
I could only fill my ears with wax,
and run rough dirt through my hands,
and when the moans ceased,
steal upon Troy's walls
to try to catch a glimpse, a glimpse
of the still standing tents and banners.

She joined me upon the high walls of Troy,

Creusa, searching for her lover, her prince,
the very son of Love, now lost in a skirmish of dust,
a dancing of swords, too far for eyes to see,
as I watched for mine. *It will be well,
it will be well*, she told me, a warm hand
upon my arm. Although I will confess –
I die a little each time he leaves the walls.
And live a little upon each return.
A gift, or curse, of the gods, this half death.
A curse, or gift, this shining life.

                Somehow, I think, I think –
                He shall live.

*That does not mean
that I shall.*

Dust, dust, in great clouds,
entering our throats. And from below,
that unending cry of swords.

They speak of nothingness. Of *void*:
that first dark chaos, where nothing moves
and nothing breathes, not even
dancing gods, who take their pleasure
in our pain. A void the immortal gods
have suppressed. A void I learned to know
all too well, too well.

You can learn to hear the sound of arrows and swords
as nothing more than the cry of birds, of cattle crying
to be milked. To wrap thick silk around the ears, to dim
the clanging sound.

But hunger, hunger.

That is harder.

They spoke, in hushed tones, of food. Of bread.
Meat. Olives. Honey. All in want, in need.
The tale of a war meant only to last a year,
or two, or three. My lover, my prince, sat,
face buried in hands and thighs. Useless, my herbs.
Useless.

If I left –

No.

If I returned –

Had you stepped outside these walls
when their black ships first crashed upon these shores,
when they kindled their first cook fires.
Had you returned –
then, then,
it might have made a difference.
Now, now –
They would not send you away.
But they are hungry, too hungry,
for our walls.

Our roof trembled
with the drumming of arrows.

EVATOS

The ninth year: that was the worst,
and yet not the worst. The return of endless,
heavy rains, turning roofs into mud
and mud into death, the cries of men
caught in heavy muds, dying beneath
a goddess' tears. Beneath the rains
lay madness, and beneath madness
death stretched out hungry hands,
and not even the endless rain
healed throats dried from crying,
or drowned out the endless scent
of death beyond and in our walls.

We gave gifts, we gave gifts, we gave gifts:
splendid creations of silver and bronze,
gold and bright gems, tripods and cauldrons,
cups and chokers, bracelets and rings,
gleaming in moon and sun. We gave gifts,
we gave gifts. Even in the midst of war,
we gave gifts, unknowing, uncaring,
that these gifts would soon rest
beneath ash and sand, gifts only to worms.

I reach for water,
tired, so tired,
of tasting fire.

Names. You want names. They named them all,
the city lords and poets, an unending knell
of endless death, retold and retold, the names
of each hero and lesser man,
fallen at the gates of Troy, the names
of the men they killed, the men that killed them.
Names I would forget, though they drum at me
in the deepest silence of the night,
when wind and sea and bird are silenced,
and the night brings only the endless list of names.

Hear them elsewhere, the names of heroes.
Hear them from another voice.

In other lands, they wrap their mortal dead
in binds of linen and perfumes, before
hiding them in rocks and sands, shelters
for their mortal ghosts. Or bury them
in unwrapped skin, in a field of mud, of dust,
marked perhaps by standing stones,
or by a patch of flowers, letting their ghosts
wander loosely upon the earth.

Here, we paused our war to burn our dead,
in part to keep their mortal bones from rising
after death, to tap upon our shoulders and drag
their fingerbones across our skin.
(*It has happened*, our nurse whispered to us,
and we shivered in delighted belief;
was I not the daughter of a swan?)
In part to loose the stench of death,
so deadly to mortal throats and minds.
In part to let their spirits rise
for one brief touch of heavenly abodes
before making their mortal ways to hell,
to the uncold shadowy realms below.

Right, it was right, to burn our dead,
and yet, every time we paused the war for this,
I dreamt of ghosts passing through my skin,
and in the morning could smell nothing but smoke.

Dry, this water that is not water.
Dry as dreams burnt
upon the feathers of eagles
stolen from the sun.

In the ninth year of war, they called
me to the high walls of Troy, as my vines
twisted ever higher upon the roofs,
and the city cried for release. They called,
and I walked on golden feet,
a purple cloak wrapped about my form,
between the swirling vines.

Below us rested men and bones,
the grinning Achaeans upon the shores,
eating of their fish and grain,
the tattered tents still holding
against the bitter wind. I shut
my eyes against the salt
that sang upon the air. The king
gestured to one tattered tent.
Who is that man? he asked.

For nine years, they had not asked –
not asked a single name of me,
nor asked me to watch this war,
fought, they said, for my name.
For the safety of myself. For the right,
they said, of women to love; for the right,
they said, for Troy to hold me within

its golden walls, to hold me
dancing within its court.
For nine years, they had not asked.
For nine years, I had not seen.

I knew the man – how could I not –
the man who had once held my sister.
And the man beside him, who had once held
my cousin, and the other men
upon that shore, who had once tried
to hold me.

I spoke that name, and many more,
my tongue soon wearied from the list of names,
the tedious tales of their many deeds,
most but tales woven of drink and pride,
though more tender to these men for that.
They brought me drink, dark wine
unmixed with water. Shaking, I sat and drank
and watched my prince stroll from the golden gates
to wait for my love, my king.

He found me in the rooftops, in the gardens.
He found me with grapes staining my skin.
The flowers watched us in silence,
as the wind whispered songs of deceit,
as he sucked honey from my breasts.

Desire, they say, had brought us to war.
And yet. War had never been part of our desire.
And I say, had all men yielded to those same desires,
the walls of Troy would never have burned.

Outside, the armies were counting my worth,
as my prince and I were lost in love,
the breath of the goddess heavy on my skin.
Payment. For a queen, and nine years of war.
Payment. For weariness, and blood,
for the cries of the spirits in the forests and seas,
begging for peace. For silence. For gifts –
gifts ungranted by men busy with swords.
Payment. What is the measure of a goddess queen,
trapped beneath a goddess's breath?
Payment. What of the gardens I had raised,
of the dances I gave for kings and courts,
of the buildings I caused to be raised against the wind,
of the songs risen in my praise?
Payment. What of the payment to me,
for being born a toy and plaything of the gods,
divine daughter stripped of divine power,
save for the light dancing on my skin,
save for the drugs my mother brewed,
ensnared in the webs of the gods?
Payment. What is the measure of a woman undivine,
trapped on the other side of the sea,
unhearing of her lover's fate,
cursing me with every morning breath?
Payment. I took my price
on my lover's skin. My prince
took his price in song. My king
stood upon the hard sand shore,
and twisted a gold coin
in his left hand.

The taste of gold
lingers on my tongue.
So cold, so cold.
And the only heat I hold.

I must fight him, my prince, my love, said,
lashing on his gold-laced greaves. *I must.*
I caught his arm. *He cannot fight. Nor
can you.* Bleakness rested in his eyes.
He is no fighter. My lover seized my lips;
wrapped twisted plates across his chest.
*They will kill you, if I
do not fight.* I tasted blood.
I am Helen, I whispered as he left.
Helen. A radiance raced
across my arm, and I climbed to
the city walls.

The sun, my cousin, my kinsman, lit my golden hair
with the fires of the sun. Below me, whispers stirred:
daughter of gods. Above me, swans sobbed.
Not songs of death, these sobs, not songs at all;
in their sobs I heard only the sounds of war.

———

Did I watch? To this day,
I cannot tell. Dust fills my throat.
I try to weep, and find no tears.
They fought, my prince and my king,
they fought, my lover and my love,
a battle that clashed into song.
And I, the reason for their fight,
cannot remember watching.

———

A dream pulls at me. I stir,
smelling the bitter smoke
of ships burning on the seashore.

———

He returned that night, my prince, my love,
wearied with dust and blood, his head
bowed beneath his heavy helmet. I called
for slaves, a bath, more water, oil:
and cleaned his skin myself
with cloths and tongue. I bound
his wounds with the softest of linen,
fetched all the way from distant Egypt,
still holding the warmth of that hotter sun.
I rubbed oil into his skin, feeling
the pain of the muscles within. I rested
lips upon his shoulders.

> *You never told me of his strength.*

> > *I thought you had the eyes
> > to see.*

> *He spoke of you.*

My lips withdrew. I moved
to the narrow window, looking upon
the lower gardens I had sown,
thinking of
my plants upon the rooftops.
Nothing more.

> *He spoke of you
> in kindness. He wished to know
> if you danced. He wished –*

My flowers would open
to the dawn, would release
their dust into the wind,
would shake beneath
the faintest breeze.

> *They will sing it otherwise,
> of course.*

> *They could not hear, and our lips*
> *were well covered by*
> *shadows and dust.*

I would stew drugs,
steam leaves, and bring
comfort and death. I would
bring dreams. I would
transform them with
the work of my hands.

> *He is well.*

Perhaps some hot wines
to ward off
the wind's harsh chill.
Perhaps.

> *I could not cut*
> *at his heart's blood.*
> *Nor could he*
> *pierce into mine.*

Warmth, warmth
filling my hands.
I pressed my lips
into his neck,
let the golden light
drift from my hands.

Know this:
A god is virgin in no tale. That fate
the goddesses reserved
for their own, whether they chose
to become ever virgin with each spring,
or to hold their virginity against all time and desire.

Sometimes I think this weakness.
Sometimes I think this strength.

———⚓———

That began the fighting
in earnest. They had warred before,
the city and the ships, in sharp and bitter raids,
and screamed their minor fights or leaped
for two warriors in a duel. They had burned
and burned and burned, and hurled
insults sharp as arrows and arrows
heavy with fire and blood. They had dug
sharp trenches to hold a fierce siege
and walls to better hold the besiegers.
But they had not *fought*, not as they fought now
as if the immortal gods breathed through their lips
utterly careless of injury or death,
rejoicing in the clash of spears and the endless shrieks,
leaping over those already embraced by death,
as if in leaping they could avoid
a touch of that icy embrace,
the taste of the cold river,
that swirled just beyond their sight.

Eris herself, they said, stalked among the men,
her voice raised in fierce war cries, eyes reddened
from the blood she drank. Fiercer even than the god of War,
they said, she would not flee the field of battle
to nurse her wounds in the arms of Love, or some other
goddess of more healing and more peace, but instead danced
among the spears and shouting men, letting her own immortal blood
fall into their mouths, until hungered, they no longer cared
for what blood might spill from their own mouths
as blow upon blow rained upon their chests.

The air, once filled with the song of dice
upon the shore, the call of sweet lyres
upon the sea, now trembled beneath

a different song: the ragged thump
of spears and shields of bronze,
the endless song of arrows,
a song no mortal could long silence
or fail to feel shuddering
inside our bones.

We clasped hands over our ears in pain,
and wrapped our heads in cloth,
and worked over the bleeding men dragged to our feet
by shouting men, and the women who dared
the crush of spears and feet
to save the wounded, those the immortals would allow
our hands to heal, as Creusa unweeping
dragged the dead from us, and lit their fires,
taking from her own small chests
coins to speed their journey, as outside the walls
the unsaved dead sank in mud as men leapt over them.

---

it should be
easier
to
forget,

but the gods
have never
been so easy.

They came to me in shadows,
my unbrothers, uncousins,
sons of immortal gods
who could claim kinship with me
and now lay unbleeding in the dust
outside the city walls, who now
in fire became that dust, their

shadows pulled beneath the earth,
to wander in the underlands. But first
they came to me, to stand
beside my silken bed, to touch
my radiant skin, to stroke
my hands and clutch
my feet in desperate grips, no more
painful than the touch of water warmed
soothing against the skin. And yet
I shuddered in pain and fear,
backing up against the wall,
clutching my soft blankets to me,
hands whitening upon the silks,
shivering under their grey hands.

They name death a man upon a pale grey horse,
a follower of my unbrother War, a brother of my
uncousins Sleep and Dream, more immortal than I;
more mortal than my sister. And yet I tell you this
who met with Death so many times: Death is not one,
but many: an old grey man in a dark cloak, a dark maiden
in a cloud of mist, a young boy smiling, holding out his hand.
Little Deaths, you name them, mere followers in his dusty train,
and so they are, but to any mortal that they touch,
as real as the Death that leads them.

We crept from the city gates beneath
night's enchanted cloak, to gather the wounded
and the dead, and scatter sweet petals,
gathered from my gardens, to cover the scent
of blood and death, from flowers I had grown
to keep the hope of love, of life,
growing someplace on our rooftops,
beneath our topless towers.

The gods themselves came then, to play
in our war, slipping between the
clanging spears, the brilliant shields,
whispering lies and painful truths,
no more than shadows, flickering
from an uncertain fire. They spoke
and warriors trembled beneath that sound;
they spoke, and armies whirled.
The cry rang out: someone had speared
immortal Love.

      It throbs, my wrist, it throbs;
      I bring it to my mouth, and feel
      the lips of my prince, my love.

When immortal Love was wounded
I felt the wound myself,
harsh upon my wrist. My arm pulsed
with hot blood, seeping from
a wound I had not taken. I pressed
my fingers against the wound,
and fled to Troy's high towers,
searching for the bright helms
of my lover and my love. I could see
nothing in the dust. The blood throbbed,
and I fell gasping. *Love, love,*
a voice murmured. *You take these
wounds for love.* A dark swirl,
a tilt of earth, and nothing more
for a time. A time.

      In memory, it bleeds.
        In darkness, it throbs.

He tended me himself, my prince, my love,

anointing the wound with a sweet salve,
and binding it with his skillful hands,
before pressing his lips against mine,
to remind me, perhaps, why I could still
so willingly take such deep wounds
for love.

Later, they said, that I fought with her, Love,
upon Troy's shining walls, watching the goddess'
enticing breasts, accusing her of trickery. A lie, a lie.
I never fought Love. Against her, I was helpless,
and Wisdom had long since abandoned me.

A goddess might summon gentle Sleep,
and bend him to her will, calling
the gods of the swelling underworld
as witness, but I, I had only the cloak of Night
to hide beneath, and it
brought no sleep, nor consolation.

Madness. My prince, my love
stood by the fire, the dust of the dead
still grim upon his cheeks. *Madness.*
The war is not enough. Now the very gods
sow confusion in our midst, snatching mortals
as we might seize an angry cat,
pulling it from the fray, though with
less concern for their shining skins.
You stab, and the target is gone;
you stand, to find yourself in a mist,
seeing nothing. They stab at
friend and foe alike.

Cool water from the city well
fell over his hair and face, leaving
ashen rivers running down
to pool upon the floor.

*I did not know the immortals had
such love for you, my love.*

Sometimes, we paused the war
to burn the dead, pulling torches from
stony temples, praying the dead might see those lights,
and with them, find the swiftest way
to the gates of hell and death's dry rivers.

It was after such a pause that the cry arose:
Achilles, tired of battling men and rivers,
calling for our prince's blood. The blood of Hector,
tamer of horses.

         Hector –

        I might have loved.
Had I seen him before my prince, my love,
Had I seen him among my fierce suitors,
I might have loved. I might have trapped him
in my arms, might have kept him from Troy's walls,
had I led him to my bed. And so I wept
as his pyre burned, as his brothers
poured cool wine over its embers,
pulling his bones from the cooling fire.
And so I wept at his feast, as golden light
poured from my hands, and my prince, my love,
sat silent at my side.

Even now, I dream, I dream,

of his dancing steps, his battle cries,
his eyes gazing over the high walls,
resting on the sullen spears. I dream
of horses dragging him through dust,
of bending to kiss his battered lips,
filling my mouth with his death dust.

The smoke still lingered when she came to me,
his mother, queen, grey and dull
in the radiance of her robes. I stood,
and inclined my head, a queen to a queen
thinking of golden Sparta, and my king,
and of the tales my prince had told.
She moved slowly, the queen, as if the very gods
held her ankles against the stone, as if she would,
with a gesture, a word, turn into the very stone
that would hold up the city, but feel
none of its blows, its fire.

Do not think I have forgotten
who it is that caused this war.
Do not think I do not know
whose name to place upon
the altar of the Furies, whose soul
to curse here and beyond,
beyond the rivers, the rivers of death.
Do not think I will forget.

>   Agamemnon, I said, not quietly,
>   letting the fire enter my throat.
>   remembering the tale of my sister, my twin,
>   the broken body upon her chest.
>   *This war is his, and no other.*

And yet your husband stands
outside our gates.

The fire died inside my throat.

If I had hoped that only Hector's heat had kept
the flames of war alive, that his dreadful death
would chill the spirits of the lords and princes
who stood in shadows about our halls,
I soon learned the truth of it. The very soils
turned red with blood, and I choked
on the endless smoke of the burning dead.

I would leave the city, I whispered to my herbs, my plants,
as his sister, his twin, stood nearby. *I would return
to the king, and end this war. If I thought
love, and fate would let me pass these gates.*

Your fate, your fate, my unsister whispered,
touching my hand with one slender finger,
her silken veil concealing her shadowed face.
*No. Bound to him you may well be
in this city, at this time. But he and I
shall both travel down to the realms of hell,
and pay the price to cross the river,
to enter the realms of dreams and death. But you –*
Another touch. *I understand it not. Nor have I seen
this fate in others. But light tells me, in its deadly sight,
You shall not leave the mortal earth
by any path, to any place,
of dead or immortal, shadow or light,
until you have learned to sing.*

Her words shook my breath, my skin.
Golden light fled from my hands.

You lie. You lie.

She shook her head beneath the silk.
If only, if only, I did.

A clatter of horses, a raining of stones. My prince
leaping through my gardens, rushing to our walls
where I stored his excess arrows. *Achilles comes.*
I shuddered. My prince's smile, once so lingering,
flashed at me. *No true concern*, he told me,
leaving a kiss upon my golden cheek
that as always swelled at his lightest touch.
I longed to pull him to my bed. My hands
reached for my sweetest herbs. *You do not
go into battle?* I asked, my hands playing
upon his chest. *No. Although* – the slightest
return of his dancing smile, the slightest press
upon my hand – *today I feel as if I could
outrun Achilles himself.* Another kiss,
a snatch of arrows, and he was gone,
leaving me amongst my herbs.
but Achilles is so swift of foot, I whispered.

If he heard me, my prince said no word,
only clambered up Troy's topless towers,
setting an arrow to his bow, hiding well behind
shields of stone and mud. I could see him,
in the way of lovers who can see their loves
in every stance apart from them, every
hidden place. I could see him lean
against the stone and mud, his arms –
oh his arms – so firm, so firm upon that bow. I
could see him swallow, see him think of songs,
of words that were his greatest gift,
think of him bantering with the trickster hero,
the very one whose vow had brought them here,
to the heat and fires of these distant shores,
could see him wishing for an exchange of songs
instead of arrows, and then with one harsh breath –

I heard the cries, the shrieks. The city stopped.
As one bright arrow from my prince's hands
entered the ankle of swift-footed Achilles.

It was no swift death such as
poets sing of. The arrow pierced
his mortal flesh, the one scrap of skin
left unbound by a mother goddess
and her magic waters. It bled slowly,
so slowly, and we heard his shrieks,
his screams of poison. (My prince
shuddered and closed his eyes. I never told him
of the drugs I made, of his princely brothers
stealing my leaves in starlit nights
when he and I were wrapped in love,
mixing their deadly powders, or how
they would smile slyly at me
and ask me for the secrets of drugs,
and how, to garner their friendship,
I whispered some of my mother's words.)
We heard the army wail their prayers
to any god that might hear; saw the very sea
rise upon the shore, shifting into a monstrous form,
shrieking its rage and anger. We knelt ourselves,
against that rage. And then we heard it:
the mourning cries, the striking of shields.
The death of Achilles, our greatest fear.
Smoke rose softly from his funeral pyre.
It drifted into our city, as a shark
slides though darker waters, its mouth
ready for blood. My prince
lifted his face, and breathed in the smoke,
not choking on the taste of death.

I lit the fires in our rooms that night;
stifled the braziers that brought us light.

We would have shadows for this.
I shall die for this, he whispered.
I knelt by his side.

                      They name you hero.

They name us all heroes. His face was dark
and twisted, though even I could not tell
if it twisted in pain or grief. *I have killed
the greatest of all of us.*

                      Your enemy.

He has sat on the shores
and watched the sea
for many a day in battle.

                      And fought you today.

You do not say we.

        Silence shimmered between us.
        The fire crackled. No god that,
        no divine spark, but I felt
        the unchill of hell
        settle upon my shoulders.

                      *I am bound and caught
                      by love, such love.*

You do not say we.

                      Because it is you who bind me.

    I caught his mouth in mine,
    dragging him to our silken bed.

                      *Because when our skins touch,
                      you become I, and I you;*

> *both more and less than we.*

He was not the one
I aimed for.

> Our teeth sunk
> into each other's flesh.
>
> We were fierce that night,
> fierce. The embers crackled
> in the fire. I left him marked
> with my hands and teeth.

Dawn woke us too early, rosy colored fingers
pulling at our eyes. I pulled him back to me
when he would leave our bed
for the less tender arms
of princes. He kissed me without heart
or mind. *Once we slew monsters*
to become heroes. Now –
now I slay Achilles, player of lyre,
slayer of Hector, tamer of horses.
The fire died in a sudden rush,
and I let my love, my prince,
weep on my chest.

> *He was not the one*
> *I aimed for.*

Shadows bind me
as I walk. I cannot
remember
if I wept.

But I remember Achilles,

his silver lyre
singing over the ocean waves,
remember his voice roaring over our walls,
as he cried for the blood of Hector,
slayer of his cousin, slayer of Trojans,
remember his shade
cursing at me
upon the steps of hell.

If this sounds unlike the men of song,
remember this:
those were the songs of men,
and this is a song of mine.

DEKATOS

The tenth year: that was the worst

                                            the utter worst.

THANATOS

They dragged my lover to me, broken,
the light far passed from his eyes, his skin
not skin, but a mere wrapping
above his broken flesh. I touched his hand.
Cold, so cold, though warmed by the sun;
still, so still, though I shook its fingers.

The blood of a swan
         pulses through my veins.

               I cannot die
       until I have learned
to sing.

It was not so fast as that,
the breaking.

The other wife. She had the gift
of healing, that I in all my immortal blood
could conjure only with my herbs. *Summon her,*
I begged. *Summon her. She still
holds a kindness, or more,
for him. Her hands hold life.*
Through the tunnels the children ran,
up through the mountains of Troy,
to the trees of Mount Ida,

calling for the other wife,
while I mixed potions near a fire,
and his sisters held his wounds.
They called, and called, and the trees
swayed in the wind, the green voices
singing, but at her fountain,
only her ashes, and a smoldering fire.

I bent over his body, his shattered body,
wanting to allow my salt drenched tears
to drench his skin, to send the dust upon his skin
flooding into the earth. But I could not weep.
I had not stopped weeping when alone,
trapped in the bed that had held us both,
in the dreary days of siege,
in the love soaked nights of song.
In that bed, I could not stop;
tears choked my throat. I could not
breathe. And yet, before him, I stood silent.

A yellow cloth of rough linen
was thrown over his body. I pounced on that,
to seize his soul from the cloth,
to have him tell me this was all a trick, a lie,
that this was the nightmare, and our lives the truth;
but the cloth slipped from my hands
and I knew my nightmare had become truth.

Empty, empty, was that night,
its goddess huddled in some distant land
offering no comfort.
Empty, empty, were my arms and eyes.
I shivered from an unfelt cold,
shivered, shivered.
From the corners, shadows whispered

all yours all yours all yours this death
and I tasted poison upon my lips.

I would have had them both in Sparta,
my lover and my love, my dancing prince
and laughing king, fed them both
on rich meats and grapes, led them to
soft silkened beds. I would have had them both
upon the stony hills, or among
the dusty vineyards, would have
taken them both to the cooling seas,
and played with dolphins in the waves,
and never heard the harsh sighs of men
caught in an arrow's deathly grasp.

I loved, how I loved,
my song is love and my life is love,
snare and breath and life and death
woven so I cannot see the separate threads,
but pulsing, pulsing with my love.

I cut my wrists until they dripped with blood,
pulsing through my golden skin. I sipped poison after poison,
placed my face in pools of water, stepped into
the kitchen fire, took my king's bright sharpened dagger
and plunged it deep into my heart. And still I lived,
and still I breathed, while about me others aged and died,
while about me Death moved on silent feet,
his shoulders shaking with laughter at my cries.

So random, this immortality. So unjust.
So undeserved. I could name
a hundred immortals who deserve it not,

a thousand – ten thousand – mortals that do.
Chance-guided, the Fates that seize us both,
mortal and immortal alike. One moment
dancing beneath the sun, the next –
bark crawling up your legs, your hands
splaying into a thousand leaves
as a god weeps at your roots. I watched
the gold shimmer upon my wrists,
and saw Death, my uncousin, my unfriend,
cloak his face against me, and heard
his laughter as he left to
wander among more mortal souls.

Later, they told me
it had not been my love, my king,
who loosed that final arrow.
A small band about my heart became undone.
I could not have borne that, not have lived
in sun or shadow, knowing my lover, my king,
had been the hand to loose
that final poisoned arrow, to know
behind his hand had rested mine,
mine the hand and heart that guided
poison into the heart of my prince, my love.

No.

It was some other, some mighty hero,
known for burning other heroes,
and stealing their weapons from their funeral pyres,
muscles shining in the cruel firelight.
He tipped his arrows in rich poison,
before sending them soaring into the sky.
One random touch, and lesser men writhed:
One random thrust, and greater men died.

Or so they said.

That too, might have been a lie.
But truth or lie, the poets sang it,
sang of the lighter of pyres and the poisoner of men,
and I held his dark image in my heart,
and lined it with thoughts of fire.

                                        Broken, broken,
              all was broken,
                      save the city walls
                                      that kept me close.

I wept, and the skies wept with me,
I called upon my cousins Hyades,
and begged them to unleash the skies,
to unleash the tears held back by clouds and suns.
Weep, I begged, *weep with me. Weep for me.*
And they, hearing my cry, my unsong,
opened their arms and hands,
and the skies joined their tears with mine.

Did you expect from me remorse? Cries of repentance, pleas
for forgiveness, for sweet mercy, for a kinder justice
than I might have earned? Poets indeed have placed
these words into my mouth, and women have claimed
that I sung such cries from the walls, the day and night
Troy burned, naming myself bearer of war, accursed,
deserving of all my griefs, of all women in Troy
the least.

I have no such cries to give, though indeed
in that final year of war, I might have agreed
with those that named me accursed.

I mixed herbs, I mixed herbs. I walked along
the dying with my golden cup of rich spiced wine,
raising their heads, lifting their lips, for one
final drink, placing my lips upon their skin,
readying them for the final flames.

Even now, a cloud of dust, a drop of blood,
and I am there upon those streets,
listening to the final sighs, the final gasps,
and the end of breath.

Sleep was cousin to me, and should
have gifted his powers to me at will,
allowing me to spend the night embraced
by dreams of shadows or shadows of dreams.
Instead, he brushed his fingers upon other eyes,
and Night, rich Nyx, brought to me no comfort.

Revelation does not always come
in a fall of fire or a storm of stones,
or even in a soft gentle flow
of water, like the lightest of fall rains,
promising a later chill.

The stars brought no comfort in the dark of night.
I heard no voice of wind or sea or bird.
I stirred my drink of drugs, allowing the clouds
to consume my mind, urging myself to no more thought
than the growth of herbs, the touch of love.
In the dark, I reached out my hand to my love, my lover, my prince, my king,

and finding nothing, threw the cup from me,
and wept, rocking in the darkness.

They would not let me die,
my blood and the city.
They would not
let me die. The knife
slipped from my hand;
poison choked
but did not kill.
They would not
let me die.
And so,
undying,
I learned of death,
the unfilled absence,
the unanswered call,
the living death that holds a room
as a true death leaves it empty.

DITHYRAMB

I did not eat. I did not sleep. I did not talk.
They lifted me, from time to time,
that they might bathe my skin
and change my robes, and poured cool water
through my cracking lips. I knew only the air,
the harshness of the hot, hot air,
so harsh that air, that I might breathe.

In the echoed silence of my mind,
I cried his name again and again.
It *burned,* his absence, *burned,*
and all my tears could not quench that fire.

Nothing. Nothing.
             All of this –

    nothing.

I spoke to any who would listen,
and many who would not. I told
the vines of each word he said, of how
he had sung of women and gods, of how
he had touched me every night, and said,
he could not live for long
without my touch. Of how
he had not lived for long
with it.

I took no breath without thought of him,
ate no meal without thinking of his voice.
And in the dark of night, I reached, I reached –
to fall when nothing was found.

                      Place me upon the ships,
                      I begged. *Send me back*
                      to my king. My hands
                      reached for Troy's high walls,
                      for the red sails that stood beyond.

The princes smiled.
      No.

                      And soon enough I lay beneath
                      the arms of another prince.

                      A woman's duty,
and Troy's pride. It would soothe my soul,
the women said, and slow my tears.
I kissed him fiercely, as if to prove
I could still live, and then,
lay still on the bed, knowing again
breath is not life, though a body's breath
may indeed mock that fate.

Give in to him, his sisters whispered.
You will forget. And so I kissed
his hardened thighs, prepared
sweet baths, dropped
honeyed dates into his mouth.
He held me as I wept and wept,

he held me when I had no tears.
He was well enough, this Trojan prince,
though when we touched I felt no more
than a crawling emptiness,
and not all his hunger for my skin
could begin to fill that void.

His absence lay heavy on my skin. I stood on the walls,
and breathed the stink of death, unable to feel him
leave my hands. Again, again, the words: *My prince, my prince.*
Sometimes I even named him, *Paris, Paris,*
before tears dissolved me. *My prince, my prince,*
and nothing, not even the knowledge of my king,
my love, waiting by the hollow ships,
could break the endless circle,
the echoed silence in my mind.

I hid myself among my mirrors,
the shimmerings of gold and bronze
that flickered back my distorted eyes
encased in coldest metal. I hid myself,
and watched myself, for some small spark,
some small glimmering mote of light
that might prove me living beyond
my own heartbeat and my own
harsh breath.

You are goddess, divine, they told me. *Mourn not.
Another owns your body. Love him,
love him, love him.* And so golden light
*rained from my ha*nds, and so I kissed his mouth,
and so I watched the darkness eat the sun,
and I wept, I wept, and wished the salt

might eat my skin.

A woman with two loves
should hope to hold one.
I had neither. Water ran clear
through my pain wracked hands.
The light seemed dark, so dark.
The hands of a stranger moved over me,
leaving bruises upon my skin.

I knew, none better, of the holes to hell,
the pathways to that mighty river, the shadows
that closed upon those ways, the gates that were not gates.
I even knew of the tricks to lure those monstrous dogs
that were not dogs, and of the coins to pay
the ferryman upon his skiff, who for a price
might take mortals and shadows alike,
across the river that was not a river, knew a dance
to dance before the queen of bones, my sister. All this
I knew.

*You cannot die
until you have learned to sing.*

My mouth opened. My fingers trembled.
I kept my feet on mortal earth
and turned my eyes to the burning sun.

O IPPOS

To build that horse, first they cut the forest
where trees had danced beneath stars and moon,
and mated with the wind, where springs
had slipped between the roots of deep trees,
to let water maidens slide between
the legs of rough tree men, and tree spirits
taste the sweetness of fresh earth water. The forest
where my lover, my prince, and I had
drunk the light of sun and stars. They cut that forest
with blades of bronze and gold, blessed
with the breath of lesser gods. The blades
tangled with the roughened woods.
They cut that forest, and the forest shrieked;
for seven sharp nights and six dark days.
The wind sobbed out every harsh name,
singing to my wounded ears, as the immortals
tumbled past, shrieking on their endless fall
to the shadowed underworld.
Seven sharp nights of their harsh cries,
of waiting for my own harsh death.

For seven sharp nights, we heard their harsh cries,
carried by the wind to our rough walls.
Children hardened by war and siege and fire
cried within their mother's arms.
Until silence: a grey dawn,
and the great horse alone upon the shore.

So odd, to see that shoreline without black ships.
Almost I begged for a feast by the sea,

a festival of fish and sun, until my eyes
met the blank stare of that terrible horse,
and I had no more taste for food.

———•———

They knew, the Trojans, how they knew
when that wooden horse surfaced
upon the shore. No work of gods, this
wooden beast, but a clumsy, ugly thing
only of mortal men. They knew
of the trickery of Greeks. They knew.
Weariness pressed upon their backs,
and with a sigh, they opened their gates.
They knew.

———•———

The smallest spark to start a warming fire.
A thousand sparks to burn a city.

———•———

When they dragged her into the sun,
Cassandra screamed. The sun's bright beams
raped her skin. Beneath its brilliant
pitiless heat, she writhed
upon the sands. And seeing this
Agamemnon smiled.
She whimpered her vision
into the sands. And naturally,
they thought she lied.

———•———

When the city burnt I let its smoke
fill my hair, my mouth. Creusa lay
beside me, dead, her mortal lungs
twisted in smoke. I, half mortal, breathed

the smoke, and felt the fire
fill my hands. I walked
through the flaming walls, and felt
alive as I had never felt
since my prince had breathed his last. I heard
his songs in the rough smoke,
and left the palace on unshod feet.

He lay in a stony street, my king, my love,
his leg cruelly pierced
by a bolt of wood. I knelt
and touched his lips with mine,
drinking in the taste of smoke,
and pulled my knife to ease the bolt
from his muscled leg. Flames
masked his screams. I tied his wound,
and lifted him,
and sought out the nearby shore.

Afterwards, I was told, a second doom
came upon the city: this a doom of raging water
sweeping down from high mountains,
crushing all in its path, taking golden halls
and roughened huts and columns
stained dark with fire and smoke,
and the wall, the great Achaean wall,
sending it all into the sea, to be swallowed
in a sudden gulp, in a rage of foam,
leaving only chaos and lesser tears behind.

A shadow falls
    across my mind. I

am resting in my
lover's ship,
clinging to
his arms,
his legs
golden Troy before us.

                I am alive, alive;
                the winds wrap me in their song.

I am free, free,
the shadows wrap me in their tears
and unsung song.

EGYPT

He came to me at sea, my king,
weeping on my breasts, he came,
and I clung to him in the salt wind.
He held me again, my love, my king,
melding his legs with mine. I knew
how to make him gasp, and with my mouth
I danced away our memories.
He kissed me again, my lover, my king,
and I thought I heard Procne weeping.

Ten years, and we still knew
how our legs should intertwine,
how his tongue should tease out mine,
how I could draw a long cry from his lips,
and he draw fire across my skin.

I dip my hands in the salted ocean,
the churning wine dark seas.
Throbbing, throbbing. I draw my hand
to my lips, and taste the salt,
and see a dimming of the gold,
a small gift from some watery kinsman.

He had touched other women, I knew,
before and after we had met, had kissed
their lips and caressed their skin,

in the long years I had spent at Troy.
It lay between us, unspoken,
and soon enough, forgotten,
save in what it had taught us both of love.

He watched me upon the ship, as I leaned
against the rails, as he slowly healed
from the thousand thousand cuts, the burns
left upon his skin by fire.

A twin, he said. *A twin.*

> Cassandra, shrieking in the night,
> beneath his brother's sword.
> My love, my prince –

>> *No.*

> *Clytemnestra?*

*Not your twin. A twin. A double. A twin –
dressed and gifted with your skin,
singing with your voice. A twin
walking the walls of Troy. I found
you in Egypt, Egypt. You were never in Troy. You
never held another, never kissed his lips
never walked on the walls to call men to battle,
nor watched women burn for Achilles.
Never.*

I traced his lips with my tongue.

> *Never.*

So sweet that lie upon our tongues.

And so we came to Egypt, to its

marshy, treacherous reeds, hiding the mouth
of its mighty river, and its river gods.

Shadows of grass near the dry river.
Shadows of song.
My feet step in the mud that is not mud.
My hands strum the harp that is not harp.
Almost, almost, I dream.

In Egypt, I learned more of drugs,
the subtle essence of crushed leaves,
of seeds and poisons and crushed flowers,
concealed in silver, and dropped in wine.
the tinctures that could, with but a drop,
shift the veil between the worlds, letting even those
of purely mortal blood taste a glimpse
of other worlds. A deadly glance,
a poisonous hint, for once seen,
the other worlds do not so easily leave
mortal minds, and another drop
may not shift those veils. *False dreams*,
said some, *shadows, no more*. And watched
my golden hands, and wept beneath
the pitiless sun.

I knew nothing of their river gods,
or their gods that moved the deadly sands,
or those that used the tongues of beasts
to speak their divine wisdom. All these
were unkin to me. Their temples
chilled my hands, the golden light
dimming in their darkness. I bent my mind
to mortal magic, mortal drugs,

and ignored the pulsing
in my hands.

Later I wondered, wondered if
all that we had heard and seen –
the whispers in the ancient trees,
the shadows flickering without sun or wind,
the faces that grinned in clashing battles
before vanishing in dust and blood –
if these were nothing more than powdered dreams,
mixed by mere mortals in a cup,
birthed by sweet teas and tiny flames,
even as I watched the golden light
swirl upon my hands, and watched
Death nod gravely from his corner,
and heard the song of immortal lyres.
Until I heard her golden laughter
and felt myself beneath her breasts:
No. I, still trapped by Love,
could hardly claim her but a dream.

Later he told me of it, my lover, my king,
as we dawdled on a rocking boat,
the river slipping away below us,
of his journeys through their sunbright temples
and shadowed halls lined with faces
of queens and gods, pharaohs and beasts, of the
sweet scent filling his nose and mouth, of bending
his ears to the wails of a cat
denied its daily treat of fish, of finding himself
unthere.

    He kissed my hand
    in memory.

> *Mist and shadows,*
> *sung into your blood*
> *by their drugs.*

Shadows shifted. His men
lay upon the sands, throats torn
by thickened teeth. A goddess laughed.
Unthere. He struggled
beneath a coat of heavy fur
crusted in salt from the
deepest seas. Shadows shifted.
Tightly he held to all he knew,
knowing all he knew were shadows.

> In my hands pulsed
> light and shadow.

>> *Only mist –*
>> *that and shadow*
>> *sung into your blood*
>> *by drugs.*

Or a moment, a moment,
inside your world.

> My hand withdrew.

> *Not mine.*

>> He watched the light spill
>> from my hand.

As you wish,
daughter of thunder.

>> No –

That was not my world, the world of drugs,

though I poured them often enough,
to seize men's minds, or heal their souls,
to bring sweet peace and sweeter dreams,
to quiet the angry roars of men. Not to open
other doors, to give false glimpses of false gods,
not when immortals walked among our halls,
laughing under mortal faces, or danced
in swaying forests, beckoning to mortal men,
ensnaring mortal women. No, I would not
mix such drugs, not in this world
where the boundaries between us
might be less than a shimmer, though
I might mix rich potions to open dreams,
to give the unaware a glimpse of other shadows,
and the seeing some respite
from the shadows resting in their eyes.
Potions I withheld from my love, my king
who had danced with too many shadows,
and still carried their marks on his skin.

Dreams and lies, lies and dreams,
and the quiet joy of a dimming sun,
as I rested, rested, leaning against the still strong arms,
of my lover, my love, my king.

RETURN

Before I left –

> *my prince, my prince, my love, my love,*
> *leaning against his chest in the wind of the sea*

    – Sparta reveled in luxury.
(Not until long after I left its city walls
did the city embrace its other path
of warrior skill and strength.) The city
melted in silks and the coolest of linens,
overflowed with the finest, sweetest foods,
the most tender meats, the richest wines
baths of hot and cold flowing water, the cold
of gold upon the feet, the air
filled with musics and perfumes,
to hide all shadows and pain. Nothing stinted,
nothing withheld, that could be cupped in our hands,
or chewed within our mouths.

So much changed when I returned, clutching the hand
of my lover, my king. Climbing the walls
we stood, gold-shining, triumphant
and looked at Sparta's dust, the greyness
that had fallen upon our streets, the buildings
that had tumbled into stone and dust,
with no one to tend them. I looked upon
the city stones, lifted my golden hands.
We will rebuild, I said. And once again
welcome lords and kings to bright golden halls,
and serve them wine in matchless cups. We
will rebuild, and leave
other cities in our dust.

The faces of our slaves and nobles alike
showed only tightness in their smiles.

My mortal father, dead, my mortal mother, vanished
in a feathered storm, or so they sang; brothers lost
to dancing shadows, and sisters fled. I placed my hand
on Sparta's stones. This, this, at least
I would not lose. I would not lose. Sparta would be mine.
Mine.

My city stirred with anger, counting the bones
left upon the sands of Troy, the heroes
lost upon the churning seas, or snatched into
a wind hungry for vengeance, or blood. They counted.
Day and night, they counted. A god
might well have removed such wounds,
such scars of grief. A god might well have
laid a veil of sweet forgetfulness, of merciful relief,
and drained away anger and tears. A god, yes.
But no god came, save only slow Chronos,
who stood in a corner and said no word.
And I – however golden my skin, whatever
the fury of gods within my blood, the pulse of immortal
that filled my heart—I could do nothing, no more than weep,
and they did not want my tears,
though their own water filled eyes
watched me with a dreadful hunger.

And now this song,
                        this bitter song.

They sang of how I left my daughter
in golden Sparta, to grow alone and friendless,

her parents both caught in passion and war
upon a distant shore. They sang of how she grew
in beauty near equal to mine, and that
she wed the son of my sister, my twin
after his madness, or before, or that
she wed the son of Achilles, after his death,
or before.

Lies, all lies. I had no daughter, though often I watched
the children of my sisters play, and held
the children of my love, my king, and watched
the children of my lover, my prince. No more.
To my mortal twin came the children:
lovely and righteous, angered and piteous,
daughters and sons.

Or so I tell myself, sitting in shadows,
heart burning, hearing the echoes
of those songs. I never had that gift,
that curse. I had no daughter, not before the war,
nor after. No daughter wed to a distant prince,
no daughter slain by her cousin in fury.
I had no daughter. Golden light
pours from my skin, leaving my hands
cold and grey, and bleeding.

She came to us after my return, my sister, my twin,
two of our sisters silent behind her,
quivering like shadows of trees
flailing from a wind. (Odd, that; she had never
named them sisters, had named only me
to her blood and kin.) *Sister*, she said,
and always her golden shadow, I knelt
before her, my lover, my king,
unbent at my side. *Sister*, I said,
and dry arms embraced, and dry cheeks touched.
Golden medallions enclosed her arms. *You must meet*

my new lord and husband, she said. The slightest
of shrugs. *I fear my daughter cannot be here
to greet her uncle. She was exchanged, you see –*
The faintest of smiles. *For your safety,
and for swifter wings.*

Horror gripped my throat, as my mortal twin
drew a slim fast finger across her own. I would have moved,
but she bared her teeth, a rat ready to gnaw
upon old bones. *Oh sister, sweet sister,* she whispered.
Her tongue grazed my ear. *Think not
that I blame you. Think not that I do not know
how the blood that you have devoured
sickens you, how you have crouched in corners,
washing your hands, coating your feet
in water and oil. Think not that I blame you
for the actions of men, for the warcries that stole
the men from our fields, the skilled hunters
from mountains, leaving olives to rot
and bees to choke in unharvested honey.*
Her hands clutched my shoulders.
*Think not that I blame you for my husband's knife,
the very knife that slashed across my daughter's throat,
its bronze gleaming in the sun.*

*They said a goddess
stole her,* whispered my lover, my king,
his lips soft upon my shoulders. *She –*
His fingers slid up and down my arm.
*She struggled. His soldiers used ropes.
The winds stayed still. They placed
a rag inside her mouth, so he
would not hear the screaming.
They placed her against
the rough stone. He raised
the knife. The winds stayed still.
He shut his eyes. A sudden scream –*

> and nothing but rope
> upon the stone. His teeth
> pushed against my skin.
> Nothing but rope, and no trace
> of blood. I thought perhaps –

You watched?

> I watched our boats, watched
> our banners slump in the
> unmoving air, and wondered if
> from those topless towers
> your eyes ever rested
> upon the sea.

Dark wine glowed in our
golden goblets. I set the
metal edges to
my lips.

> I thought perhaps –
> one of your brothers. Even then,
> the men told tales of
> shadows on the edge, of two men
> flickering from shadow to light.
> They had the skill, I thought. But
> others spoke of something green.
> A flicker, no more, of radiant green,
> a wild breath, the taste of blood,
> woman, all woman. They knelt.
> And rising saw only the broken ropes
> against the stone, and no trace
> of footprints. Only the knife
> quivering in the stone, and
> the howl of joyful winds. His lips
> pressed my forehead. *She lives,
> my love, she lives.*

And your brother –

> *has died for it.*

The wine felt bitter
upon my tongue.

In the morning light
her face was bitter, bitter,
stripped of its silver
left grey by the night.

> (*Wake the trees,*
> *wake the trees,*
> *and the leaves shaking*)

I myself served her
the finest of breads,
the sweetest of wines,
ordered slaves to oil her skin
and dress her in my own soft silks,
my sheerest linens from Egypt.
I knelt at her feet, and played my lyre,
with all the subtlety taught to me
by my prince, my lover

> (*fingers and laughing and*
> *ah, ah, it should be eased by now, eased,*
> *not this –*)

I wiped her tears
as she spoke of her children

> *missing*

and sat with her watching
the hearthfire smolder.
Sister. Her fingers pierced mine,

but I did not cry out.

I cannot have her here. The voice of my lover, my king,
filled not with pain, but truth. *My warriors
will turn upon us three, will slit our throats
in the brightness of day, if I shelter the one
who killed my brother. Sister or not.* His hands
lay lightly upon his knees. *I did not ask you
to welcome those who killed your own brothers,
who laughed as they spilled dark blood. I cannot.*

                        She alone has not blamed me.

Not she alone.

                                  In the silence
                             the fire crackled.
                I felt the shadows
        stealing closer.

I weave a swift curtain
between life and death,
the whispers of the dead
dancing in my ear.
Never are my fingers
swift enough.

                Shadows, shadows,
fragile echoes of her dulcet tones,
her warnings and tauntings in my ear,
the rumors of her son's swift twisting knife,
the memory of two young girls,
leaping merrily among the forest rocks,

the memory of my attempts to sing.

Later, her daughter cursed
my very name, singing of
her sisters broken, her father slain,
her brother run mad
with bitter guilt. Later, later:
for now I defied my king, my love
and plied my sister, my twin,
with the broken comfort I could give.
For now I watched upon the walls,
as she rode, my sister, my twin,
for her own fate, and darker songs.
For now, I returned to wait
in my room made warm with rich cloths,
and brood upon my city. Mine.

Sparta. Sparta. Golden Sparta –
You at least were mine, all mine,
ascending from the broken stone and mud.
Triumphant. Renewed. Golden.
And mine. My one creation left upon mortal earth,
and my one creation left unsung.

The harp of copper and bone trembles in my hands.
My mouth is dry. I place my fingers upon the strings,
and watch the dancing shadows.

We built. We planted. We planned. I wove –
my hands and loom forever working,
forever clacking beneath my will.

We must have splendid gifts again,
fit for kings and more than kings. Men came to us,
one by one, broken, weeping, dreaming of fire,
and we brought them wine from our own sweet hills,
brightened by my own brewed drugs. We built.
Sparta glistened in music and art,
reveled in luxury and tales. Wanderers came
to our golden court, to be feasted with the richest wines,
dark bread well laced with the matchless oil
of Sparta's hills, meats fresh hunted
from our forests and mountains,
to hear tales told and retold,
to tell tales told and retold,
until by the telling some small sorrow
might be put to rest in a shallow grave,
even as the others brooded at the mind's edge
ready to pounce, and devour.

I heard the whispers in the streets. *Most evil of women.*
The names of the fallen, the tales of the men
who would not return. I heard the whispers
of relief, of praise. *She has ended the war, ended it.*
We shall have no more battles for years. I saw
Death in a corner, laughing. I heard the other whispers,
other words. *She has caused the war, caused it:*
I shall no longer embrace my son again. I saw
the turned faces, the cool looks that counted
the bones left at Troy. *Not I*, I said, but not aloud.
Not I. I knew nothing of that dark vow.
And I was hardly the only treasure they wanted.
          They needed a target, and I – I shone.

A silver harp placed in my hands,
by my lover, my king.

> *I cannot sing.*

But your fingers have such skill.

> *fires, fires, the stink of death*

> *I cannot sing.*

His hand laced within my own.
It is not I who need to hear your song.

My fingers trembled on the strings.

We have gods to propitiate, said my king, my love,
his hand playing within my own. *A city to build.
A city of temples.* His eyes hunted mine. *Perhaps –
perhaps – upon that highest rock –
you may raise a temple to love.*

I shivered in the heat of the sun, and heard
the thunder rage in nearby hills. *No.
That rock –* I thought my throat
filled with stones. *That rock –*
My tongue could not have thickened so,
in but a glance at Sparta's rocks.
*To me it calls to Wisdom. It can be
a quiet place to weave, to watch
the slow growth of olive trees upon the hills.*
Some immortal finger touched my neck.
In the hills, the thunder lessened.

In my rooms, I shiver, shiver.
The fire fills the air,
but does not touch my skin.

I built temples to every immortal of our hills –
save Eris alone, who laughed upon our walls,
and threw her bloody bones at me. Small and great,
their temples gleamed, or burst with brilliance,
as singers sang seduction and acclaim.
And for the thunder, a temple of gold,
facing the sky defiant. My father's anger
rumbled in the hills, and I laughed, welcoming the rain.

And for Love, sweet Love –
her raging touch still lingered upon my skin.
And so for her a temple upon the hills,
and a second altar deep within nearby mountain caves,
where any could descend, and be overwhelmed by Love.

Later, for me, they built the smallest of shrines –
Little more than a pile of rocks upon a hill –
and sent their daughters there, still clutching dolls
so that they might sing of Helen.

They told me of the city songs,
of the songs sung throughout the hills.

They say a god cursed your father's line
with daughters sworn to infidelity. They say
you and your twin cannot love, but only lust;
that you and your sisters can bring nothing
but grief to this earth.

      my prince, my lover, singing with his harp –

           I am the daughter of thunder.

*His daughters, too,
have been cursed to grief,
and bringing grief.*

    Love envelops me as a heavy snow
    uniting cold and beauty.
    Love. My skin aches. I tremble.

I would you returned to your father's skies.

        the arms, the hands of my love, my king –

          I have never known the way.

They stop me in the streets of Sparta,
to tell me of the lost: the men, the women
who boarded the ships of my king, my love
to follow me across the wine dark seas.
They stop me to tell me their many tales.
They themselves do not stop. Or forget.

A song trembles in my hands,
a phoenix huddled
beneath the ocean.

And so the years passed, in despair and peace,
as mortals blessed and cursed my name.
My love, my king, grew grey and rough,
with the years of wind and sands. And I –
I still stood golden, slim, as time
laughing, danced around my path.

He watched me, my love, my king,

watched as I danced unchanging,
and held me as I wept with pain,
as mortal agony laced through me,
that not all my golden skin could heal.

So much I had lost. So much.
So much I had built. So much.
So much I had lived. So much.

                                                Empty, empty,
a sky stripped of bird and star and moon and sun.

DAEMON

They came last night, he said, my love,
my king, his hair grey in the dying light,
as evening drew its shadows. *They came. Voices –
voices heard through silver light,
thickened with honeyed shadows.
They came.*

        I stirred a honeyed drink
        over hot flames.

*It will not be long,
my love, my queen.*

        The flames roared. Hot liquid
        sprayed upon my skin.

                I did
        not burn. I could not burn.
        Not upon my skin.

They come.

              Was I not
        mortal as he? My golden hands
        trembled in the dying light.
        Did I not bleed dark mortal blood,
        crave the bread made by mortal cooks,
        sip upon mortal wines?

*My love, my love.
they come.*

>   The honeyed drink slid
>   into two cups. I brought them
>   to my king, my love, sat
>   upon our bed, the bed of olive wood
>   carved by immortal hands, graced
>   by weavings made by mortal hands.
>   Slowly we drank. The shadows
>   edged ever closer. In the corner,
>   Death inclined his head.

Would you could
make me immortal
with a kiss.

>   I placed golden hands
>   upon his chest, felt the light
>   pulse within them. I bent
>   my lips to his, and *willed*
>   the light to enter,
>   though his mortal skin
>   resisted my touch.

Come. His tongue
still urgent upon mine,
his hands –

>   No.
>   I would not lose this.
>   I would not.

Let me feel immortal
in other ways.

>   I would not feel the world
>   break beneath my hands again.

———

I paused at the edge of the olive groves,

where the trees sang softly in the wind,
and waited, for the wind and the mingling of stars and sun,
and waited, for my brother to tell me of death.
No mortal word, I heard the night winds whisper,
as they gathered for their starlit dance.
No mortal word.

I am not mortal,
I whispered back, and waited in the grove.

His shadow twisted when he came,
risen from the corn rich earth. Only a shadow:
I could not tell which brother stood by me
and which had slipped past us both
to take his turn within the earth. I lifted
my golden arms and a shining torch,
and stepped towards my brother's shadow.

I cannot die, it seems. The shadow flickered in the wind.
And yet I would not live alone. The trees sang of silver mists.
My throat tightened. *I am love,* I confessed.
The trees laughed in the wind. *Tell me how to keep this love.*
Tell me how to make the trade. The shadow bent to my ear.

———

Stones. So cold these stones.
So dry this river.
So grey my hands,
so cold, so cold.

———

And in my ear, the whispered song.
And in my hand, a golden apple.
And upon my shoulders, a grey cloak.

———

Gold pours from my hands,
and all is grey, grey.
Shadows hold me, and in their touch,
I hear the faintest songs
from a harp of bone and blood.

I passed them upon my return,
the maidens digging my ungrave,
singing as they dug and placed
smooth stones around the tiny hill.
Goddess, they named me, goddess,
weeping for my golden hair,
weeping for my beauty's blood,
planting dark roses upon its earth,
a place for quiet worship and unquiet dance.
I watched, and watched, and opened my lips –
but it was not yet time for song.

So thin his breath, when I returned
pale and grey as any ghost,
wrapped in a cloak of finest clouds.
So pale his face. So tight his fists
against some hidden pain. So eager
his lords about his bed,
to take my city in their hands.

They did not part for me, those lords
holding to their valiant wall of mortal limbs
to guard against the approach of Death.
But I saw Death, unkin to me,
standing at the entrance of our hall,
and as I passed, he bowed to me,
and followed. Our grey hands moved
through the line of men and lords.
They shivered in our chill. I knelt

beside our bed of olive wood
and took his hand, my king, my love,
and raised my voice in song.

———

voices voices voices

                                        Have I fallen?

                                        Have I fallen?

voices raised in song and war

        voices raised in despair

voices raised in joy.

                                        I stand.

———

Golden drops fall from my grey skin,
staining his lips a brighter bronze.
Behind me and Death, the warriors gasp,
fall to the stony floor on softened knees.

                        I sing, I sing.

He rises, my king, my love.
His skin glitters with borrowed gold.
I toss a cloak of dreams and death,
woven from the ashes of a golden ram,
so soft between my trembling hands.

———

You were the
daughter of thunder,

the golden queen.

You might have feasted
among the gods. Or,
dancing in shadowed lands,
followed your lover into death.

                                      So I might.

His fists clench.
Perhaps against some hidden pain.
Perhaps against the gold upon his skin.

Swift, swift, the curtain that I weave,
from the shadows cast by Death.

Swift, swift the spread of golden lace,
swift, swift the growth of shadows.

Grey, grey, the hand I extend,
to my love, my king.

Bright, bright, Death's laughter,
as he takes my hand.

Grey, grey the shadows that arise,
as they flee, the lords of men.

Soft, soft, the roll of thunder,
echoing in distant hills.

Gold, gold, the branch that trembles
in my cold grey hand.

I do not see them leave, the lords of men,
though I hear them weeping, hear them tell my city
that thunder has called their king and queen,

called them to the shining halls,
and so passes an age of heroes.

And still, and still, I sing.

Asphodel and light,
pomegranate seeds stained with red.
Harps of bone and blood and copper,
the silent shadows of the trees.

A shimmer. My prince, my love,
a shadow against the shadowed trees,
one hand raised against a laughing wind,
gone more swiftly than the ring of laughter.

Gates of ivory and horn. A crone
laughing at red bones. Bent heroes
gripping golden coins. Women waiting, waiting,
their heads turned for their coming children.

It is not too late, daughter of thunder.

> I do not turn.
> *But it is, it is.*
> *Or early.*

I have eaten my fill of dreams and lies.
And so I pull him into shadow.

Night's sorceries rage about our throats.
We may not eat, we may not drink,
but we may touch. We may dance,
and speak with shadows and with gods.
We roam, we roam, past the dry rivers,
past the land of mists and dreams,

past the ever dancing dead, and the land
where Sisyphus toils his eternal task,
and to the thundering halls of the golden gods,
to dance and dance, and even to more mortal lands,
where in shadows now we sing.

www.ingramcontent.com/pod-product-compliance
Lightning Source LLC
Chambersburg PA
CBHW021107080526
44587CB00010B/416